TRADITIONAL SCOTTISH COOKERY

SHEILA MACRAE
with Carolyn Humphries

foulsham
LONDON • NEW YORK • TORONTO • SYDNEY

foulsham

The Publishing House, Bennetts Close, Cippenham,
Berkshire, SL1 5AP, England

ISBN 0-572-02685-4

Printed in Great Britain by
St Edmundsbury Press Ltd, Bury St Edmunds, Suffolk

Contents

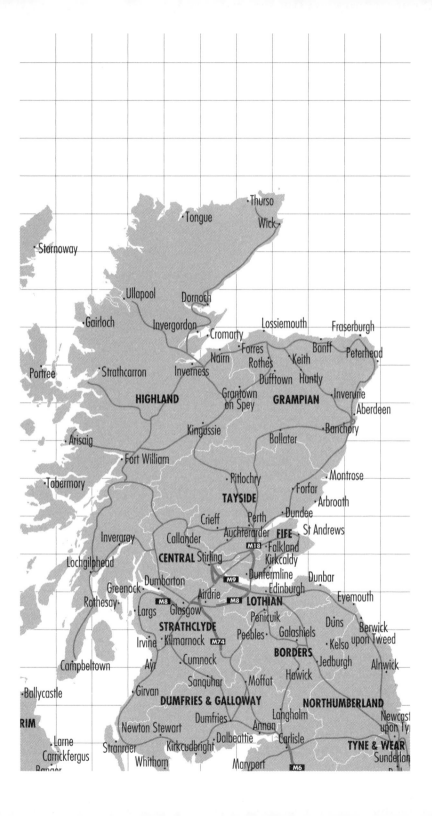

Introduction

The availability of new ingredients and the range of ready-made foods now sold in the supermarket has broadened the scope of everyone's cooking and extended their horizons way beyond what is traditional in their own region. But that very progress lends a nostalgic magic to those treasured, old-fashioned dishes. In the case of Scottish cookery, there are many Scots who are all the more determined that the heritage of their country's traditional fare shall not be be forgotten. There are very few Scottish grandmothers who don't enjoy making old-fashioned clootie dumplings or bairns who don't love to eat them! Recipes, hints and tips have been passed from parent to child for generations and we hope that this book will play its part in reviving those special dishes of childhood. Perhaps it will also help Scots to link hands across the vast distances that sometimes divide them and introduce others to the delights of Scottish cookery.

Those who understand Scotland know it is a country with wonderful supplies of first-class game and the best beef and sweetest honey in the world. It has fruit, cereals and fish enough to give any creative cook a rich seam of ideas to mine. The basic theme running through so much Scottish cooking is using those high-quality local ingredients to create down-to-earth, nourishing and wholesome meals. With their tendency to lead an outdoor life in many rural areas, and the need for warmth in an unpredictable climate, the Scots know that these homely meals make sense. Try the Cock-a-leekie Soup (see page 54) on a winter's day and you'll understand. And as we learn more about the health-promoting qualities of fresh vegetables, fruits and traditional Scottish ingredient oats, we know we are in safe hands. Add to that the fact that the canny Scots cook is thriving in today's budget-conscious times, and meals made with a small selection of the best ingredients can be made with the minimum of effort, and it is clear that nothing could be more modern in appeal than the Scottish approach.

We have attempted the impossible and divided Scotland into six culinary regions to help our visitors identify with the particular areas and their specialities. For some of the more traditional dishes, it was difficult to trace their origins. The more popular favourites – such as Stovies (see page 65) and Black Bun (see page 120) for example – are well established over the whole country and some overlaps are inevitable. However, we hope that the selections we have made will give those who do not know the country a little insight into the best ingredients and styles from each of the regions.

Some of these recipes are fun, some economical and some exciting, but each one is a little part of Scotland to create in your own home. If you are a Scot, there is surely no better way to celebrate St Andrew's Night on 30 November and Burns' Night on 25 January than to serve some traditional dishes for your friends and family.

These lines from our immortal Selkirk Grace say it all:

Some hae meat that canna eat,
And some wad eat that want it;
But we hae meat, and we can eat,
And sae the Lord be thankit.

Notes on the Recipes

- Do not mix metric, imperial and American measures. Follow one set only.
- American terms are given in brackets.
- All spoon measurements are level: 1 tsp = 5 ml;
                                      1 tbsp = 15 ml.
- Eggs are medium unless otherwise stated. If you use a different size, adjust the amount of liquid added to obtain the right consistency.
- Always wash, peel, core and seed, if necessary, fresh foods before use. Ensure that all produce is as fresh as possible and in good condition.
- Seasoning and the use of strongly flavoured ingredients, such as onions and garlic, are very much a matter of personal taste. Taste the food as you cook and adjust seasoning to suit your own taste.
- Although traditional Scottish cooks would use ground white pepper, to suit modern tastes we have called for freshly ground black pepper in many cases as this gives the best flavour.
- Always use fresh herbs unless dried are specifically called for. If it is necessary to use dried herbs, use half the quantity stated. Chopped frozen varieties are much better than dried. There is no substitute for fresh parsley and coriander (cilantro).
- Can and packet sizes are approximate and will depend on the particular brand.
- Always preheat the oven (unless using a fan-assisted oven) and cook on the centre shelf unless otherwise specified. All ovens vary, so cooking times have to be approximate.
- Lard (shortening) or dripping is most often used for greasing and frying (sautéing). Use a good-quality oil, such as sunflower or corn oil, if you prefer.
- All preparation and cooking times are approximate and should be used as a guide only.

The Highlands

This is a spectacular land, steeped in history and legend. Everything about it has a tale to tell, for here you can find some of the oldest mountains and, it is said, the wisest people. Its most famous inhabitant has to be our elusive Loch Ness monster – and there isn't a true Scot who doesn't believe in her!

The Highlands are the majestic home of the deer, and Highland venison dishes are second to none. The people who live here are of a hardy nature but the winters are very harsh, so it is not surprising that local recipes are substantial and full of nourishment. The mouth-watering Scotch Broth (see page 10) and Clootie Dumpling (see page 24) are well-established favourites.

Scots Oatmeal Porridge

*Traditionally, Scots sprinkle their porridge with salt before eating,
but for variety you can serve it with milk and brown sugar, golden
(light corn) syrup, single (light) cream or grated nutmeg. Soak the
oatmeal in the water overnight, if you wish. If you prefer to use
rolled porridge oats instead of oatmeal, use similar quantities but
cook the porridge for only about 5 minutes.*

SERVES 2

	METRIC	IMPERIAL	AMERICAN
Water	500 ml	17 fl oz	2¼ cups
Medium oatmeal	50 g	2 oz	½ cup
A large pinch of salt			

1 Bring the water to the boil in a large, heavy saucepan.
Sprinkle in the oatmeal and salt, stirring with a wooden
spoon to stop lumps forming. Continue to simmer and stir
constantly for about 5 minutes or until the oatmeal has
absorbed the water.

2 Turn down the heat, cover and simmer for
10–20 minutes, stirring frequently. Porridge should
be thick but creamy, so add more boiling water if
necessary.

☼ **Preparation and cooking time:** 30 minutes

Scotch Broth

There are numerous versions of this delicious soup but this is a particularly good one. Some recipes use a small joint of lamb and add large potatoes; the broth is served first, and then the meat and potatoes afterwards.

SERVES 4

	METRIC	IMPERIAL	AMERICAN
Scrag end of mutton or lamb, trimmed of excess fat	450 g	1 lb	1 lb
Water	1.5 litres	2½ pts	6 cups
Pearl barley	25 g	1 oz	2 tbsp
Onions, chopped	2	2	2
Small swede (rutabaga), coarsely grated	½	½	½
Carrot, grated	1	1	1
Leeks, sliced	3	3	3
Salt and freshly ground black pepper			
Shredded kale	60 ml	4 tbsp	4 tbsp
Chopped fresh parsley	30 ml	2 tbsp	2 tbsp

1 Put the meat in a large saucepan with the water and pearl barley. Bring to the boil, reduce the heat, skim the surface, cover and simmer gently for 1½ hours until the meat is really tender.

2 Lift the meat out of the pan, remove the meat from the bones, chop and return to the pan.

3 Add all the remaining ingredients except the kale and parsley. Bring to the boil, reduce the heat, cover and simmer for 30 minutes.

4 Add the kale and simmer for a further 15 minutes. Taste and adjust the seasoning. Sprinkle with the parsley before serving.

⏱ **Preparation and cooking time:** 2¼ hours

Nettle and Barley Broth

Make sure you gather your nettles from an unpolluted source, away from roadways or animals.

SERVES 4

	METRIC	IMPERIAL	AMERICAN
Pearl barley	75 g	3 oz	scant ½ cup
Chicken stock	1.2 litres	2 pts	5 cups
Bouquet garni sachet	1	1	1
Young nettles, finely chopped	225 g	8 oz	8 oz
Large potato, diced	1	1	1
Salt and freshly ground black pepper			

1 Bring the barley, stock and bouquet garni to the boil in a large saucepan, cover and simmer gently for 1 hour until the barley is tender.

2 Add the nettles and potato, return to the boil, cover and simmer for about 20 minutes until all the ingredients are tender. Remove the bouquet garni and season to taste before serving.

⏲ **Preparation and cooking time:** 1½ hours

Haggis

*Although not many people will make their own haggis, a Scottish
cookery book could hardly be complete without this most famous of
recipes. Traditionally, haggis is stuffed into a sheep's paunch before
boiling. This modern-day version uses a roaster bag tied at both
ends to make a sausage shape instead.*

SERVES 4

	METRIC	IMPERIAL	AMERICAN
Lamb's heart	*1*	*1*	*1*
Lambs' liver	*100 g*	*4 oz*	*4 oz*
Large onion	*1*	*1*	*1*
Shredded (chopped) beef suet	*75 g*	*3 oz*	*¾ cup*
Medium oatmeal	*225 g*	*8 oz*	*2 cups*
Salt	*10 ml*	*2 tsp*	*2 tsp*
Freshly ground black pepper	*2.5 ml*	*½ tsp*	*½ tsp*
Beef stock	*300 ml*	*½ pt*	*1¼ cups*

*Rich Gravy (page 13), Tatties (page 45), and
Bashed Neeps (page 45), to serve*

1 Mince (grind) the heart, liver and onion, or chop finely
in a food processor.

2 Place in a bowl and stir in the suet, oatmeal, salt,
pepper and stock to give a wet consistency.

3 Tie one end of a roaster bag with a metal twist tie.
Spoon in the mixture and twist the other tie to close, leaving
a 2.5 cm/1 in air gap in the bag to allow for expansion.

4 Bring a large pan of water to the boil. Drop in the
haggis, cover, reduce the heat and boil for 3 hours, topping
up with boiling water as necessary.

5 Lift the haggis out of the pan. Carefully open the bag
and tip the haggis out on to a warm serving plate.

6 Serve with Rich Gravy, Tatties and Bashed Neeps.

🕐 **Preparation and cooking time:** 3¼ hours

Rich Gravy

SERVES 6

	METRIC	IMPERIAL	AMERICAN
Large onions, chopped	2	2	2
Carrots, diced	2	2	2
Butter or margarine	25 g	1 oz	2 tbsp
Caster (superfine) sugar	5 ml	1 tsp	1 tsp
Plain (all-purpose) flour	25 g	1 oz	¼ cup
Beef or lamb stock	600 ml	1 pt	2½ cups
Bouquet garni sachet	1	1	1
Salt and freshly ground black pepper			
Gravy block or browning (optional)			
Whisky	15 ml	1 tbsp	1 tbsp

1 Fry (sauté) the onions and carrots, in the butter or margarine in a saucepan for 5 minutes, stirring, until golden.

2 Add the sugar and continue to fry for 5 minutes until a rich brown.

3 Stir in the flour and cook for 1 minute.

4 Remove from the heat and gradually blend in the stock, then add the bouquet garni. Return to the heat, bring to the boil, reduce the heat and simmer for 10 minutes.

5 Remove the bouquet garni sachet, then strain through a sieve (strainer), pressing the vegetables firmly with a wooden spoon to extract the maximum flavour.

6 Add seasoning and a little gravy block or browning, if liked. Stir in the whisky, reheat and serve.

🕐 **Preparation and cooking time:** 30 minutes

Highland Hare Cakes

SERVES 4

	METRIC	IMPERIAL	AMERICAN
Boneless hare meat	225 g	8 oz	8 oz
Fat belly pork, rinded	100 g	4 oz	4 oz
Slices of stale white bread	2	2	2
Butter or margarine	50 g	2 oz	¼ cup
Small onion, chopped	1	1	1
Mushrooms, chopped	50 g	2 oz	2 oz
Paprika	1.5 ml	¼ tsp	¼ tsp
Salt and freshly ground black pepper			
Eggs, beaten	1–2	1–2	1–2
Dried breadcrumbs	100 g	4 oz	1 cup
Melted lard (shortening) or oil	30 ml	2 tbsp	2 tbsp
A little celery salt			

1 Mince (grind) the meats together, or chop them finely, and mix together thoroughly.

2 Soak the bread in cold water until soft, then squeeze well and mix in with the meat.

3 Melt half the butter or margarine and fry (sauté) the onion, mushrooms and paprika for about 3 minutes until softened but not browned.

4 Stir the onion mixture into the meat, season with salt and pepper, and use enough of the egg to bind to a firm mixture. Shape into cakes about 4 cm/1½ in thick. Dip the cakes in the remaining egg, then the breadcrumbs to coat.

5 Heat the lard or oil in a frying pan (skillet) and fry the cakes for about 10 minutes until well-browned on both sides.

6 Blend the remaining butter or margarine with celery salt and pepper to taste. Place a knob of the flavoured butter on the top of each hare cake and serve.

🕐 **Preparation and cooking time:** 20 minutes

Venison Patties

These patties can be eaten either hot or cold. Traditionally, they would be made with home-made rough puff pastry (paste), but you can use ready-made shortcrust (basic pie crust) or puff pastry, if you prefer.

SERVES 4

	METRIC	IMPERIAL	AMERICAN
Cooked venison, finely chopped	*225 g*	*8 oz*	*2 cups*
Allspice	*5 ml*	*1 tsp*	*1 tsp*
Salt and freshly ground black pepper			
Prunes, stoned (pitted)	*100 g*	*4 oz*	*⅔ cup*
Port	*150 ml*	*¼ pt*	*⅔ cup*
Strong beef stock	*300 ml*	*½ pt*	*1¼ cups*
Rough puff pastry	*225 g*	*8 oz*	*8 oz*
A little milk or beaten egg, to glaze			

1 Season the venison with allspice, salt and pepper.

2 Simmer the prunes in the port for 10 minutes, then chop the fruit and add to the meat with the port and stock.

3 Roll out the pastry on a lightly floured surface. Use half to line four Yorkshire pudding tins (pans) and make lids from the remainder.

4 Spoon the meat mixture into the pastry cases (pie shells). Dampen the edges of the pastry, add the lids and seal together, fluting the edges. Glaze with milk or beaten egg.

5 Bake in a preheated oven at 220°C/425°F/gas mark 7 for 15–20 minutes, then reduce to 375°F/190°C/gas mark 5 for 40 minutes or until the pastry is golden and cooked through and the filling piping hot.

🕐 **Preparation and cooking time:** 1¼ hours

Roast Venison

Large joints of venison should always be marinated – preferably for as much as two days – before cooking, to make the meat tender and flavoursome. If you cannot buy rowanberry jelly (clear conserve), use cranberry, redcurrant or blueberry jelly instead.

SERVES 8

	METRIC	IMPERIAL	AMERICAN
Olive oil	*90 ml*	*6 tbsp*	*6 tbsp*
Large onion, sliced	*1*	*1*	*1*
Carrots, sliced	*2*	*2*	*2*
Burgundy or claret	*750 ml*	*1¼ pts*	*3 cups*
Garlic cloves, halved	*2*	*2*	*2*
Bay leaf	*1*	*1*	*1*
Haunch or saddle of venison	*2.75 kg*	*6 lb*	*6 lb*
Butter or margarine	*25 g*	*1 oz*	*2 tbsp*
Olive oil	*30 ml*	*2 tbsp*	*2 tbsp*
Bacon, rinded and diced	*225 g*	*8 oz*	*8 oz*
Salt and freshly ground black pepper			
For the sauce:			
Plain (all-purpose) flour	*15 ml*	*1 tbsp*	*1 tbsp*
Butter or margarine	*15 g*	*½ oz*	*1 tbsp*
Port	*150 ml*	*¼ pt*	*⅔ cup*
Rowanberry jelly	*15 ml*	*1 tbsp*	*1 tbsp*
Braised celery or chestnut purée, to serve			

1 To make the marinade, heat 60 ml/4 tbsp of the oil in a frying pan (skillet) and fry (sauté) the onion and carrots for about 5 minutes until softened but not browned.

2 Transfer the vegetables to a non-metallic dish and add the burgundy or claret, garlic and bay leaf. Put the meat into the marinade, cover and leave in a cool place for two days, turning regularly so that all the surfaces are coated.

3 Remove the meat from the marinade and pat dry on kitchen paper (paper towels).

4 Put the marinade in a saucepan and boil until reduced by half.

5 Heat the butter or margarine and the remaining oil in a heavy-based, flameproof casserole (Dutch oven), add the bacon and fry until crisp. Add the venison and fry until browned on all sides. Strain the reduced marinade over the meat and season to taste with salt and pepper.

6 Cover the pan and bake in a preheated oven at 160°C/ 325°F/gas mark 3 for 3 hours until completely tender. Remove the meat from the pan and keep it warm while you make the sauce.

7 Discard any fat from the meat juices, then boil rapidly to reduce by half. Blend together the flour and the butter or margarine and stir, a little at a time, into the sauce with the port and rowanberry jelly until thickened and smooth.

8 Slice the venison and serve with braised celery or chestnut purée, with the sauce served separately.

⏱ **Preparation and cooking time:** 3½ hours plus marinating

Civet of Venison

SERVES 4

	METRIC	IMPERIAL	AMERICAN
Beef dripping	15 g	½ oz	1 tbsp
Plain (all-purpose) flour	50 g	2 oz	½ cup
Salt and freshly ground black pepper			
Venison, cut into cubes	700 g	1½ lb	1½ lb
Bacon rashers (slices), rinded and chopped	2	2	2
White wine vinegar	15 ml	1 tbsp	1 tbsp
Port	150 ml	¼ pt	⅔ cup
Beef stock	600 ml	1 pt	2½ cups
Onions, chopped	2	2	2
Black peppercorns	3	3	3
A few chestnuts, peeled (optional)			
Mushrooms, sliced	50 g	2 oz	2 oz
Seasonal vegetables, to serve			

1 Melt the dripping in a large flameproof casserole dish (Dutch oven). Place half the flour in a shallow bowl and season with salt and pepper. Toss the venison and bacon in the seasoned flour, shaking off any excess. Fry (sauté) in the dripping until well-browned all over. Remove the meat from the pan.

2 Spoon off all but 15 ml/1 tbsp of the fat, then mix in the reserved flour and cook for 2 minutes, stirring until browned. Stir in the vinegar and port until blended, then add the stock and bring to the boil, stirring continuously. Skim the fat off the surface, if necessary, then season to taste with salt and pepper.

3 Return the meat and bacon to the pan with the onions, peppercorns and chestnuts, if using. Cover with a well-fitting lid and simmer for 2 hours.

4 Add the mushrooms and continue to simmer for a further 30 minutes until the meat is very tender. Serve with seasonal vegetables.

🕐 **Preparation and cooking time:** 2½ hours

Highland Steak

SERVES 4

	METRIC	IMPERIAL	AMERICAN
Butter or margarine	*50 g*	*2 oz*	*¼ cup*
Fillet steaks	*4*	*4*	*4*
Double (heavy) cream	*45 ml*	*3 tbsp*	*3 tbsp*
Scotch whisky	*30 ml*	*2 tbsp*	*2 tbsp*
Salt and freshly ground black pepper			
Strong hard cheese, grated	*50 g*	*2 oz*	*½ cup*
Chopped fresh parsley	*30 ml*	*2 tbsp*	*2 tbsp*
Mashed potatoes and a green vegetable, to serve			

1 Melt the butter or margarine and fry (sauté) the steaks until cooked to your liking – about 2 minutes each side for rare, and longer for well done. Transfer to a warmed serving dish and keep warm.

2 Pour the cream and whisky into the pan and heat through until almost boiling, stirring in all the meat juices. Season to taste with salt and pepper.

3 Pour the sauce over the meat, sprinkle with the cheese and parsley and serve with mashed potatoes and a green vegetable.

🕐 **Preparation and cooking time:** 10 minutes

Partan Pie

SERVES 4

	METRIC	IMPERIAL	AMERICAN
Large cooked crab	1	1	1
Grated nutmeg	1.5 ml	¼ tsp	¼ tsp
Made mustard	5 ml	1 tsp	1 tsp
Double (heavy) cream	30 ml	2 tbsp	2 tbsp
White wine vinegar	45 ml	3 tbsp	3 tbsp
Fresh white breadcrumbs	75 ml	5 tbsp	5 tbsp
Salt and freshly ground black pepper			
Butter, melted	25 g	1 oz	2 tbsp

1 To prepare the crab, pull the body and legs away from the top shell. Remove the bundle of intestines either stuck in the shell or clinging to the body. Scrape the bundle to remove any dark meat still clinging to it, then discard it. Discard the gills (dead men's fingers) from the body.

2 Scoop out the dark meat from the shell into a saucepan.

3 Twist off the legs and claws, crack and pick out all the white meat. Add to the saucepan.

4 Pick out the little bits of white meat from the body (this is fiddly). Add to the pan.

5 Mix in the nutmeg, mustard, cream, vinegar and 30 ml/2 tbsp of the breadcrumbs. Season to taste. Heat through, stirring.

6 Wash the shell and pack the mixture back into it. Mix the remaining breadcrumbs with the melted butter and sprinkle over the surface.

7 Place under a preheated grill (broiler) until golden brown on top. Serve straight away.

🕐 **Preparation and cooking time:** 30 minutes

Partan Bree

SERVES 4

	METRIC	IMPERIAL	AMERICAN
Large cooked crab	1	1	1
Milk	600 ml	1 pt	2½ cups
Long-grain rice	50 g	2 oz	¼ cup
Chicken or vegetable stock	450 ml	¾ pt	2 cups
Anchovy essence (extract)	5 ml	1 tsp	1 tsp
Tomato purée (paste)	10 ml	2 tsp	2 tsp
A pinch of salt			
White pepper			
Single (light) cream	120 ml	4 fl oz	½ cup
Chopped fresh parsley, to serve			

1 Prepare the crab (see page 20). Pick all the brown and white crab meat out of the body and small legs of the crab. Crack the large claws, remove the meat, cut into neat slices and put to one side.

2 Put the milk and rice in a saucepan and bring to the boil, then reduce the heat and simmer gently for about 15 minutes until the rice is really tender, stirring occasionally.

3 Pour into a blender or food processor and add the brown and white meat from the body and small claws. Purée until smooth.

4 Return to the saucepan and stir in the stock, anchovy essence and tomato purée. Season to taste. Reheat until almost boiling, then stir in the cream and the sliced claw meat. Taste and adjust the seasoning if necessary. Do not allow to boil.

5 Ladle into warm bowls and sprinkle with parsley before serving.

🕐 **Preparation and cooking time:** 45 minutes

Highlanders

These delicious biscuits (cookies) have a crunchy sugared edge.

SERVES 4

	METRIC	IMPERIAL	AMERICAN
Caster (superfine) sugar	50 g	2 oz	¼ cup
Butter or margarine	100 g	4 oz	½ cup
Semolina (cream of wheat)	50 g	2 oz	⅓ cup
Plain (all-purpose) flour	150 g	5 oz	1¼ cups
Demerara sugar	30 ml	2 tbsp	2 tbsp

1 Cream together the caster sugar and butter or margarine, then blend in the semolina and flour. Knead gently until smooth.

2 Roll into a sausage shape, then roll in the demerara sugar until evenly coated. Cut into thick slices and arrange on a greased and floured baking (cookie) sheet.

3 Bake in a preheated oven at 180°C/350°F/gas mark 4 for about 30 minutes until lightly golden.

4 Leave on a wire rack to cool.

🕒 **Preparation and cooking time:** 40 minutes

Hattit Kit

This is a rich and creamy Scottish dessert.

SERVES 4

	METRIC	IMPERIAL	AMERICAN
Buttermilk	*600 ml*	*1 pt*	*2½ cups*
Fresh milk	*300 ml*	*½ pt*	*1¼ cups*
Caster (superfine) sugar	*15 ml*	*1 tbsp*	*1 tbsp*
Grated nutmeg or ground cinnamon	*1.5 ml*	*¼ tsp*	*¼ tsp*
Double (heavy) cream	*300 ml*	*½ pt*	*1¼ cups*

1 Warm the buttermilk slightly, then add half the fresh milk, cover and leave to stand at room temperature for 12 hours.

2 Stir in the remaining fresh milk and leave to stand for a few hours more until the milk begins to solidify on the top, leaving the liquid whey at the bottom.

3 Lift off this curd and drain it through a fine sieve (strainer). Press it into a small pot and chill until firm.

4 Turn out, sprinkle with the sugar and spice and serve with double cream.

⊕ **Preparation and cooking time:** 5 minutes plus standing and chilling

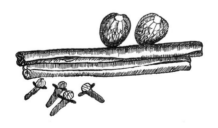

Clootie Dumpling

These dumplings were traditionally steamed in a cloth but it is simpler to steam them in a pudding basin. They are also good served cold, sprinkled with caster (superfine) sugar.

SERVES 6

	METRIC	IMPERIAL	AMERICAN
Self-raising (self-rising) flour	100 g	4 oz	1 cup
Shredded (chopped) beef suet	100 g	4 oz	1 cup
Fresh white breadcrumbs	50 g	2 oz	1 cup
A pinch of salt			
Mixed (apple-pie) spice	2.5 ml	½ tsp	½ tsp
Ground ginger	2.5 ml	½ tsp	½ tsp
Ground cinnamon	2.5 ml	½ tsp	½ tsp
Caster sugar, plus extra for dusting	100 g	4 oz	½ cup
Currants	50 g	2 oz	⅓ cup
Sultanas (golden raisins)	50 g	2 oz	⅓ cup
Raisins	50 g	2 oz	⅓ cup
Semolina (cream of wheat)	25 g	1 oz	3 tbsp
Egg, beaten	1	1	1
Milk	250 ml	8 fl oz	1 cup
Black treacle (molasses)	15 ml	1 tbsp	1 tbsp
Golden (light corn) syrup	15 ml	1 tbsp	1 tbsp
Carrot, grated	1	1	1
Cooking (tart) apple, grated	1	1	1
Plain (all-purpose) flour, for dusting			
Hot custard, to serve			

1 Mix together all the dry ingredients and fruit. Add the egg and milk, stirring well to form a dough, then stir in the remaining ingredients.

2 Turn into a greased 1.2 litre/2 pt/5 cup pudding basin. Cover with a double thickness of greased greaseproof (waxed) paper or foil, twisting and folding under the rim to secure.

3 Stand the basin on a plate or saucer in a large saucepan and pour in enough boiling water to come halfway up the sides of the basin. Cover and steam for 3 hours, topping up with boiling water as necessary.

4 Turn out carefully on to a heated serving dish and dredge with caster sugar. Serve with hot custard.

🕐 **Preparation and cooking time:** 3½ hours

Cream Crowdie

SERVES 6

	METRIC	IMPERIAL	AMERICAN
Medium or coarse oatmeal	100 g	4 oz	1 cup
Double (heavy) cream	600 ml	1 pt	2½ cups
Sweet sherry	45 ml	3 tbsp	3 tbsp
Caster (superfine) sugar	15 ml	1 tbsp	1 tbsp
A few fresh raspberries, to decorate (optional)			

1 Toast the oatmeal in a heavy-based frying pan (skillet), tossing until golden brown. Tip out of the pan.

2 Whip the cream, sherry and sugar until softly peaking.

3 Fold in all the 15 ml/1 tbsp of the oatmeal. Spoon into serving dishes and sprinkle with the remaining oatmeal. Decorate with a few raspberries, if liked.

🕐 **Preparation time:** 10 minutes

Dornoch Dreams

SERVES 4

	METRIC	IMPERIAL	AMERICAN
Butter or margarine	50 g	2 oz	¼ cup
Water	175 ml	6 fl oz	¾ cup
Plain (all-purpose) flour	100 g	4 oz	1 cup
Eggs, beaten	3	3	3
Raspberries, whole or lightly crushed	350 g	12 oz	12 oz
Clear Scottish heather honey	100 g	4 oz	⅓ cup
Drambuie	30 ml	2 tbsp	2 tbsp
Double (heavy) cream, whipped	300 ml	½ pt	1¼ cups
Icing (confectioners') sugar, to decorate			

1 Melt the butter or margarine in a saucepan with the water. Remove from the heat, stir in the flour and beat until the mixture forms a ball and leaves the edges of the pan clean. Gradually add the eggs a little at a time, beating well between each addition.

2 Spoon the pastry (paste) into a large piping bag fitted with a plain nozzle (tip) and pipe 12 round cakes on to a lightly greased baking (cookie) sheet.

3 Cook in the centre of a preheated oven at 200°C/400°F/gas mark 6 for 20–30 minutes until golden brown. Pierce the buns to allow the steam to escape and leave to cool.

4 Mix the raspberries with the honey. Stir the Drambuie into the whipped cream. Split the buns and fill with the raspberries and cream. Dust with a little icing sugar and serve immediately.

⏲ **Preparation and cooking time:** 1 hour plus cooling

Fochabers Gingerbread

This gingerbread is best left for a day or two in an airtight container to mature.

SERVES 4

	METRIC	IMPERIAL	AMERICAN
Plain (all-purpose) flour	450 g	1 lb	4 cups
Sultanas (golden raisins)	100 g	4 oz	⅔ cup
Currants	100 g	4 oz	⅔ cup
Ground almonds	75 g	3 oz	¾ cup
Chopped mixed (candied) peel	75 g	3 oz	½ cup
Mixed (apple-pie) spice	5 ml	1 tsp	1 tsp
Ground ginger	5 ml	1 tsp	1 tsp
Ground cinnamon	2.5 ml	½ tsp	½ tsp
Butter or margarine	225 g	8 oz	1 cup
Caster (superfine) sugar	100 g	4 oz	½ cup
Black treacle (molasses), warmed	225 g	8 oz	⅔ cup
Eggs	2	2	2
Bicarbonate of soda (baking soda)	5 ml	1 tsp	1 tsp
Beer	300 ml	½ pt	1¼ cups

1 Mix all the dry ingredients together in a large bowl.

2 Cream together the butter or margarine and sugar, then stir in the warmed treacle. Break in the eggs, one at a time, beating well after each addition. Stir into the dry ingredients.

3 Dissolve the bicarbonate of soda in the beer and mix thoroughly into the dough.

4 Pour the mixture into a greased and lined 20 cm/8 in cake tin (pan) and bake in a preheated oven at 150°C/300°F/gas mark 2 for 1¾ hours until a metal skewer inserted in the centre comes out clean. Cool slightly, then turn out on to a wire rack to cool completely.

⊘ **Preparation and cooking time:** 2 hours

Ginger Shortbread

To make traditional butter shortbread, simply sprinkle with caster (superfine) sugar while still hot instead of making the ginger icing (frosting).

SERVES 4

	METRIC	IMPERIAL	AMERICAN
Plain (all-purpose) flour	175 g	6 oz	1½ cups
A pinch of salt			
Butter or margarine	100 g	4 oz	½ cup
Caster sugar	50 g	2 oz	¼ cup
For the ginger icing:			
Icing (confectioners') sugar	25 g	1 oz	3 tbsp
Butter or margarine	50 g	2 oz	¼ cup
Ground ginger	5 ml	1 tsp	1 tsp
Golden (light corn) syrup	15 ml	1 tbsp	1 tbsp

1 Place the flour and salt in a bowl, then gradually rub in the butter or margarine until the mixture resembles fine breadcrumbs. Stir in the sugar and knead to a smooth ball.

2 Roll out on a lightly floured surface to 1 cm/½ in thick, then place in a greased and lined 20 cm/8 in sandwich tin (pan). Crimp the edges with your fingers and prick all over with a fork.

3 Bake on a low shelf of a preheated oven at 150°C/ 300°F/gas mark 2 for about 1 hour or until pale golden brown. Cool on a wire rack.

4 To make the ginger icing, heat all the ingredients in a small saucepan and blend well until melted. When smooth, pour over the warm shortbread and leave to set. Cut into slices when cold.

⏲ **Preparation and cooking time:** 1¼ hours

Atholl Brose

Often served as a drink, this can be made into a delicious syllabub-like pudding. Pour into wine glasses, top with a thick layer of lightly whipped cream, lightly sweetened with icing (confectioners') sugar, and chill. Decorate with toasted oatmeal before serving.

SERVES 8

	METRIC	IMPERIAL	AMERICAN
Medium oatmeal	100 g	4 oz	1 cup
Water	600 ml	1 pt	2½ cups
Clear Scottish heather honey	30 ml	2 tbsp	2 tbsp
Scotch whisky	200 ml	7 fl oz	scant 1 cup

1 Put the oatmeal in a bowl. Stir in the water and leave to stand for 1 hour.

2 Pour into a fine sieve (strainer) over a bowl and press the oatmeal with the back of a wooden spoon to extract all the moisture. Discard the oatmeal.

3 Stir in the honey and whisky and pour into a whisky bottle (or other clean, screw-topped bottle) and store for up to 2 months in a cool, dark place. Shake well before serving the liqueur in small glasses.

Preparation time: 5 minutes plus soaking

Oatmeal Posset

A nice touch is to omit the nutmeg and put a cinnamon stick in each mug. Use it to stir the hot posset before drinking and between sips.

SERVES 2

	METRIC	IMPERIAL	AMERICAN
Milk	600 ml	1 pt	2½ cups
Medium oatmeal	15 g	½ oz	2 tbsp
Salt	1.5 ml	¼ tsp	¼ tsp
Clear Scottish heather honey	10 ml	2 tsp	2 tsp
Brandy or whisky	15 ml	1 tbsp	1 tbsp
Grated nutmeg, to taste			

1 Put the milk in a saucepan and add the oatmeal and salt. Bring to the boil, stirring, then remove from the heat and leave to stand for 10 minutes.

2 Strain the liquid through a sieve (strainer) into a clean saucepan, pressing the oatmeal firmly to extract as much liquid as possible.

3 Stir in the honey, brandy or whisky and nutmeg to taste. Reheat until almost boiling, stirring all the time. Pour into mugs and serve.

⏲ **Preparation time:** 10 minutes plus standing

The Grampians

The Grampians are a hunter's paradise; visitors from all over the world come to these heather moors in search of the famous grouse. This important bird tastes its finest when cooked simply and carefully. Roast Grouse (see page 40) has undoubtedly become one of our prime national dishes, served at Scottish reunions for decades. Hare and venison are also in plentiful supply, as is fresh fish from the North Sea.

Many of the largest clans have their castle seat in these impressive lands and down the years the Grampian cooks have revealed the splendid secrets of their ancestors' tables. The selection here ranges from the wholesome Moray Pie (see page 42) and Rumblethumps (see page 46) to Scottish Crumpets (see page 51) and Tipsy Lady Cake (see page 49).

Finnan Haddie Loaf

SERVES 4

	METRIC	IMPERIAL	AMERICAN
Finnan haddock	350 g	12 oz	12 oz
Milk	300 ml	½ pt	1¼ cups
Butter or margarine	65 g	2½ oz	scant ⅓ cup
Mushrooms, finely chopped	50 g	2 oz	2 oz
Dried breadcrumbs	50 g	2 oz	½ cup
Chopped fresh parsley	10 ml	2 tsp	2 tsp
Eggs, beaten	2	2	2
A pinch of dried mixed herbs			
Salt and freshly ground black pepper			
Plain (all-purpose) flour	20 g	¾ oz	3 tbsp
Snipped fresh chives, to garnish			

1 Place the fish and half the milk in a saucepan and simmer gently for about 5 minutes until the fish is tender.

2 Lift the fish from the liquid, remove any bones and skin and flake the flesh. Reserve the liquid.

3 Melt 50 g/2 oz/¼ cup of the butter or margarine in a saucepan. Add the mushrooms and fry (sauté) for 1 minute, stirring. Remove from the heat.

4 Combine the haddock with the breadcrumbs, parsley, eggs and dried herbs, seasoning to taste with salt and pepper. Pack the mixture into a greased 1 litre/1¾ pt/4¼ cup pudding basin to within 2.5 cm/1 in of the rim. Cover with a greased lid or ovenproof plate and bake in a preheated oven at 190°C/375°F/gas mark 5 for about 50 minutes or until firm and golden brown.

5 Meanwhile, blend the flour with the remaining milk in a saucepan. Stir in the reserved fish milk and the remaining butter or margarine. Bring to the boil and cook for 2 minutes, stirring all the time. Season to taste.

6 Turn out the loaf on to a warmed serving plate and spoon a little of the white sauce over. Sprinkle with the snipped chives and serve with the remaining sauce.

🕐 **Preparation and cooking time:** 1 hour

Potted Grouse

SERVES 4

	METRIC	IMPERIAL	AMERICAN
Cooked grouse meat, finely minced (ground)	225 g	8 oz	2 cups
Butter, melted	175 g	6 oz	¾ cup
Garlic clove, crushed	1	1	1
Dried mixed herbs	5 ml	1 tsp	1 tsp
Salt and freshly ground black pepper			
Fingers of hot toast, to serve			

1 Mix together the minced meat, half the butter, the garlic, herbs, salt and pepper until well blended.

2 Press the mixture firmly into small pots, making sure there are no air holes.

3 Pour the remaining melted butter over to seal the tops, then leave to cool and chill for 24 hours.

4 Serve with fingers of hot toast.

🕐 **Preparation time:** 15 minutes plus chilling

Aberdeen Herrings

SERVES 4

	METRIC	IMPERIAL	AMERICAN
Herrings, cleaned	4	4	4
Butter or margarine	65 g	2½ oz	scant ⅓ cup
Small onion, finely chopped	1	1	1
Mushrooms, finely chopped	50 g	2 oz	2 oz
Fresh white breadcrumbs	50 g	2 oz	1 cup
Dried mixed herbs	2.5 ml	½ tsp	½ tsp
Lemon juice	2.5 ml	½ tsp	½ tsp
Salt and freshly ground black pepper			
Medium oatmeal	15 ml	1 tbsp	1 tbsp

1 Remove the heads from the fish, then split them open and place skin-side up on a board. Run your thumb up and down each backbone two or three times to loosen it, then remove together with any fine bones.

2 Melt 40 g/1½ oz/3 tbsp of the butter or margarine in a pan and fry (sauté) the onion until softened but not browned. Add the mushrooms and fry gently for 1 minute.

3 Remove from the heat and stir in the breadcrumbs, herbs, lemon juice and salt and pepper.

4 Divide the stuffing into four portions, spread one portion over the flesh of each herring and fold the sides of the fish together again. Place in a shallow, buttered ovenproof dish.

5 Melt the remaining butter or margarine and brush it over the fish. Sprinkle with the oatmeal, cover and bake at 375°F/190°C/gas mark 5 for about 25 minutes, removing the lid for the last 5 minutes to allow the fish to brown.

⏱ **Preparation and cooking time:** 30 minutes

Cullen Skink

Cullen is the small town on the Moray Firth where this soup (skink) originated.

SERVES 4

	METRIC	IMPERIAL	AMERICAN
Finnan haddock	1	1	1
Onion, chopped	1	1	1
Milk	600 ml	1 pt	2½ cups
Salt and freshly ground black pepper			
Mashed potato	100 g	4 oz	4 oz
Butter or margarine	25 g	1 oz	2 tbsp
Single (light) cream	30 ml	2 tbsp	2 tbsp

1 Wash the haddock, then place in a shallow saucepan and just cover with boiling water. Add the onion to the pan and simmer for 5 minutes or until the fish is tender and turns opaque.

2 Remove the haddock, discard the skin and bones and flake the flesh.

3 Return the bones to the pan of liquid, bring to the boil, then reduce the heat, cover and simmer for 1 hour, then strain this stock.

4 Pour the stock into a clean pan and add the flaked fish, milk and salt and pepper to taste and bring to the boil. Add enough potato to make a creamy consistency. Gradually stir in the butter or margarine and cream, and blend all the ingredients together. Do not allow to boil.

5 Serve in warm soup bowls.

⊘ **Preparation and cooking time:** 1¼ hours

Aberdeen Toasties

This is also good made with smoked haddock. For a non-fluffy version, simply beat the whole egg and stir into the sauce with the cheese and seasoning.

SERVES 4

	METRIC	IMPERIAL	AMERICAN
Haddock fillet, skinned	*175 g*	*6 oz*	*6 oz*
Milk	*175 ml*	*6 fl oz*	*⅓ cup*
Plain (all-purpose) flour	*15 g*	*½ oz*	*2 tbsp*
Strong hard cheese, grated	*25 g*	*1 oz*	*¼ cup*
Egg, separated	*1*	*1*	*1*
Salt and freshly ground black pepper			
Slices of toast, buttered	*4*	*4*	*4*

1 Put the haddock and 150 ml/¼ pt/⅔ cup of the milk in a saucepan. Bring to the boil, reduce the heat, cover and cook for about 5 minutes or until it flakes easily with a fork.

2 Lift the fish out and flake.

3 Blend the flour with the remaining milk and stir into the milk in the saucepan. Bring to the boil and cook for 2 minutes, stirring until thick.

4 Stir in the cheese, egg yolk and fish and season to taste, then heat through.

5 Whisk the egg white until stiff and fold in with a metal spoon. Put the toast on the grill (broiler) rack.

6 Spoon the fish mixture on top and place under a hot grill until lightly browned. Serve straight away.

⏲ **Preparation time:** 15 minutes

Pickled Herrings

SERVES 6

	METRIC	IMPERIAL	AMERICAN
Herrings, cleaned	6	6	6
Salt and freshly ground black pepper			
Bay leaves	2	2	2
Black peppercorns	5 ml	1 tsp	1 tsp
Whole pickling spices	5 ml	1 tsp	1 tsp
Malt vinegar	150 ml	¼ pt	⅔ cup
Water	150 ml	¼ pt	⅔ cup
Onion, sliced into rings	1	1	1
Boiled potatoes and a green salad, to serve			

1 Cut the heads off the fish, then open out the fish and place, skin-sides up, on a board.

2 Run your thumb along each backbone two or three times, to loosen. Turn the fish over and remove the backbones and any other bones. Cut off the fins and tails. Wash and pat the fish dry on kitchen paper (paper towels) and season with salt and freshly ground black pepper.

3 Roll up from the tail to the head end. Lay the bay leaves in an ovenproof dish and pack the herrings on top.

4 Mix together all the remaining ingredients, pour over the fish and cover with a lid or foil. Bake in a preheated oven at 180°C/350°F/gas mark 4 for about 45 minutes or until the fish is tender.

5 Leave until cold, then drain and serve with boiled potatoes and a green salad.

⏲ **Preparation and cooking time:** 1 hour plus cooling

Jugged Hare

If you prefer a thicker casserole, blend together 15 g/½ oz/1 tbsp butter or margarine with 15 ml/2 tbsp plain (all-purpose) flour, stir into the sauce after step 7 and heat for a further 10 minutes.

SERVES 4

	METRIC	IMPERIAL	AMERICAN
Plain (all-purpose) flour	50 g	2 oz	½ cup
Salt and freshly ground black pepper			
Young hare, jointed	1	1	1
Beef dripping or lard (shortening)	50 g	2 oz	¼ cup
Onion, sliced	1	1	1
Carrots, sliced	2	2	2
Turnip, diced	1	1	1
Beef stock	750 ml	1¼ pts	3 cups
Bouquet garni sachet	1	1	1
Bay leaf	1	1	1
Port	150 ml	¼ pt	⅔ cup
Redcurrant jelly (clear conserve)	15 ml	1 tbsp	1 tbsp
Fresh white breadcrumbs	60 ml	4 tbsp	4 tbsp
Shredded (chopped) suet	30 ml	2 tbsp	2 tbsp
Chopped fresh parsley	10 ml	2 tsp	2 tsp
A pinch of dried mixed herbs			
Egg, beaten	1	1	1
Mashed potatoes, peas and redcurrant jelly, to serve			

1 Season the flour with salt and pepper, then toss the hare joints in the flour. Shake off any excess flour and reserve it.

2 Heat the dripping or lard in a frying pan (skillet) and fry (sauté) the joints until browned on all sides. Transfer to a casserole dish (Dutch oven).

3 Add the vegetables to the pan and fry until lightly browned, sprinkling in a little of the seasoned flour to absorb any excess fat. Transfer to the casserole and pour over the stock. Add the bouquet garni and bay leaf, cover and cook in a preheated oven at 150°C/300°F/gas mark 2 for 2½–3 hours until tender.

4 Remove the casserole from the oven. If possible, leave to cool, then chill overnight, then lift off any fat that has risen to the surface and discard the herbs. If you are serving straight after cooking, simply skim off the fat and discard the herbs.

5 Stir in the port and redcurrant jelly, season to taste with salt and freshly ground black pepper.

6 Blend together the breadcrumbs, suet, parsley, mixed herbs and beaten egg and season to taste with salt and pepper. Roll into small dumplings and arrange around the top of the casserole.

7 Cook in a preheated oven at 150°C/300°F/gas mark 2 for about 20 minutes.

8 Serve with mashed potatoes, peas and redcurrant jelly.

◷ **Preparation and cooking time:** 3½ hours

Roast Grouse

It is traditional to leave the giblets in the bird to add flavour and keep them moist.

SERVES 4

	METRIC	IMPERIAL	AMERICAN
Butter or margarine	100 g	4 oz	½ cup
Salt and freshly ground black pepper			
Young grouse, with giblets	2	2	2
Bacon rashers (slices), rinded	4	4	4
Plain (all-purpose) flour	15 ml	1 tbsp	1 tbsp
Chicken stock	300 ml	½ pt	1¼ cups
Red wine	45 ml	3 tbsp	3 tbsp
A small bunch of watercress, to garnish			
Mashed potatoes and seasonal vegetables, to serve			

1 Blend half the butter or margarine with some salt and pepper and place inside the birds' cavities. Truss the birds with cook's string and wrap with bacon, covering the breasts well. Place them on a rack or trivet in a roasting tin (pan) and dot with the remaining butter or margarine.

2 Roast the grouse in a preheated oven at 220°C/425°F/gas mark 7 for about 20 minutes, basting several times during cooking, until the juice runs clear.

3 Remove the bacon, transfer the birds to an ovenproof serving dish and return to the oven to brown while you make the gravy.

4 Pour off any excess fan from the roasting tin. Add the flour to the remaining cooking juices and cook over a low heat, gradually stirring in the stock and wine. Bring to the boil, then boil for 2–3 minutes. Season to taste with salt and pepper.

5 Garnish the grouse with the watercress and serve with the gravy, mashed potatoes and seasonal vegetables.

🕐 **Preparation and cooking time:** 45 minutes

Skirlie

This oatmeal and onion dish also makes a good accompaniment to meat and game stews. It can be used to stuff meat or poultry, too.

SERVES 4

	METRIC	IMPERIAL	AMERICAN
Beef dripping	50 g	2 oz	¼ cup
Onion, chopped	1	1	1
Medium oatmeal	100 g	4 oz	1 cup
Salt and freshly ground black pepper			
Tatties (page 45) and Bashed Neeps (page 45), to serve			

1 Melt the dripping in a heavy frying pan (skillet) and fry (sauté) the onion for 3 minutes until softened.

2 Add the oatmeal and continue to fry gently for about 10 minutes, stirring from time to time until the oatmeal is well cooked, crisp and light brown. Season well with salt and pepper.

3 Serve hot with Tatties and Bashed Neeps.

🕐 **Preparation and cooking time:** 20 minutes

Moray Pie

SERVES 4

	METRIC	IMPERIAL	AMERICAN
Butter or margarine	50 g	2 oz	¼ cup
Minced (ground) beef	450 g	1 lb	1 lb
Carrots, grated	2	2	2
Onions, chopped	2	2	2
Beef stock	300 ml	½ pt	1¼ cups
A pinch of dried mixed herbs			
Salt and freshly ground black pepper			
Potatoes, scrubbed	450 g	1 lb	1 lb
Chopped fresh parsley	15 ml	1 tbsp	1 tbsp

1 Melt half the butter or margarine and fry (sauté) the minced beef until browned.

2 Stir in the carrots and onions and fry for a further 3 minutes. Stir in the stock and herbs and season with salt and pepper. Bring to the boil, then reduce the heat and simmer for 20 minutes until the meat is tender.

3 Meanwhile, cook the potatoes in boiling, lightly salted water for about 20 minutes until tender. Drain and leave until cool enough to handle. Remove the skins and cut into slices about 1 cm/½ in thick.

4 Spoon the meat into a casserole dish (Dutch oven) and arrange the potatoes on top. Melt the remaining butter or margarine and brush over the potatoes. Place in a preheated oven at 180°C/350°F/gas mark 4 for about 30 minutes until piping hot and browned on top. Serve sprinkled with parsley.

⏱ **Preparation and cooking time:** 1 hour

Aberdeen Sausage

You may prefer to place the sausage in a roaster bag, tying it firmly at each end with twist ties.

SERVES 4

	METRIC	IMPERIAL	AMERICAN
Sausagemeat	450 g	1 lb	1 lb
Minced (ground) beef	450 g	1 lb	1 lb
Bacon, rinded and finely chopped	100 g	4 oz	4 oz
Fresh white breadcrumbs	225 g	8 oz	4 cups
Worcestershire sauce	15 ml	1 tbsp	1 tbsp
Salt and freshly ground black pepper			
Egg, beaten	1	1	1
Green salad, to serve			

1 Mix together the sausagemeat, minced beef, bacon and half the breadcrumbs. Season with Worcestershire sauce, salt and pepper and bind together with the egg.

2 Shape into a roll and wrap in a clean pudding cloth, tying the ends securely.

3 Steam over a large saucepan of water for 1½ hours, topping up with boiling water as necessary, then leave until cool enough to handle.

4 Toast the remaining breadcrumbs in a dry frying pan (skillet) until golden.

5 Remove the cloth from the sausage and roll in the breadcrumbs, pressing them gently into the sides. Leave to cool.

6 Serve sliced, with a green salad.

◔ **Preparation and cooking time:** 1¾ hours plus cooling

Scotch Eggs

SERVES 4

	METRIC	IMPERIAL	AMERICAN
Eggs	9	9	9
Cold water	15 ml	1 tbsp	1 tbsp
Pork sausagemeat	700 g	1½ lb	1½ lb
A pinch of ground mace			
Salt and freshly ground black pepper			
Fresh white breadcrumbs	100 g	4 oz	2 cups
Plain (all-purpose) flour	30 ml	2 tbsp	2 tbsp
Oil, for deep-frying			

1 Place eight of the eggs in a large saucepan and cover with water. Bring to the boil, then simmer for 10 minutes. Drain, cover with cold water and leave until cool, then remove the shells.

2 Beat the remaining egg with the measured water.

3 Season the sausagemeat with mace, salt and pepper and divide into eight pieces. Flatten each piece.

4 Toast the breadcrumbs in a dry frying pan (skillet) until golden.

5 Mix the flour with a little salt and pepper.

6 Dip the hard-boiled eggs in the seasoned flour, then, using dampened hands, shape the sausagemeat around the cooked eggs, pressing it on evenly. Roll the sausage-covered eggs in the beaten egg and then roll in the breadcrumbs once more, pressing them gently into the meat.

7 Heat the oil until a cube of day-old bread browns in 30 seconds and deep-fry the eggs for about 5 minutes until golden brown on all sides and the sausagemeat is cooked through. Drain and serve hot or cold.

⏲ **Preparation and cooking time:** 30 minutes

Tatties

SERVES 4

	METRIC	IMPERIAL	AMERICAN
Potatoes, scrubbed	700 g	1½ lb	1½ lb
Butter or margarine	50 g	2 oz	¼ cup
Single (light) cream	45 ml	3 tbsp	3 tbsp
Salt and freshly ground black pepper			

1 Place the potatoes in a saucepan and cover with salted water. Bring to the boil, then simmer for about 20 minutes until tender. Drain and remove the skins.

2 Mash the potatoes with the butter or margarine and cream, seasoning to taste with salt and pepper.

🕐 **Preparation and cooking time:** 25 minutes

Bashed Neeps

Turnips were traditionally used for this recipe, but swede (rutabaga) is often used nowadays instead.

SERVES 4

	METRIC	IMPERIAL	AMERICAN
Turnips, diced	450 g	1 lb	1 lb
Butter or margarine	50 g	2 oz	¼ cup
A pinch of ground mace			
Salt and freshly ground black pepper			

1 Place the turnips in a saucepan and cover with salted water. Bring to the boil, then cover and simmer for about 15–20 minutes until tender. Drain thoroughly.

2 Mash the turnips with the butter or margarine, seasoning to taste with mace, salt and pepper.

Preparation and cooking time: 20 minutes

Rumblethumps

An Aberdeen dish with a delightful name meaning 'mixed together', this can be served as a main course or to accompany a meat dish.

SERVES 4

	METRIC	IMPERIAL	AMERICAN
Potatoes, thickly sliced	450 g	1 lb	1 lb
Butter or margarine	100 g	4 oz	½ cup
White cabbage, sliced	450 g	1 lb	1 lb
Onions, chopped	2	2	2
Single (light) cream	45 ml	3 tbsp	3 tbsp
Salt and freshly ground black pepper			
Cheddar cheese, grated	75 g	3 oz	¾ cup
Snipped fresh chives	15 ml	1 tbsp	1 tbsp

1 Cook the potatoes in boiling salted water for about 10 minutes until tender, then drain and mash with 15 g/½ oz/1 tbsp of the butter or margarine.

2 Cook the cabbage in a very little water in a covered pan for about 5 minutes until just cooked. Drain off any excess water.

3 Melt the remaining butter or margarine in a heavy-based saucepan and fry (sauté) the onions for 2 minutes until softened but not browned. Stir in the potatoes, cabbage and cream and season to taste with salt and pepper.

4 Transfer the mixture to a flameproof dish and sprinkle with the cheese. Place under a hot grill (broiler) for a few minutes until browned.

5 Serve sprinkled with chives.

🕐 **Preparation and cooking time:** 25 minutes

Scotch Pancakes

These are sometimes called drop scones. You can use self-raising (self-rising) flour and omit the soda and cream of tartar if you prefer.

MAKES ABOUT 16

	METRIC	IMPERIAL	AMERICAN
Plain (all-purpose) flour	100 g	4 oz	1 cup
Caster (superfine) sugar	15 ml	1 tbsp	1 tbsp
Bicarbonate of soda (baking soda)	5 ml	1 tsp	1 tsp
Cream of tartar	5 ml	1 tsp	1 tsp
Egg, beaten	1	1	1
Buttermilk	150 ml	¼ pt	⅔ cup
Lard (shortening), for greasing			
Butter, margarine or whipped cream and jam (conserve), to serve			

1 Sift the flour, sugar, bicarbonate of soda and cream of tartar into a bowl. Gradually add the beaten egg and the buttermilk. Beat well with a wooden spoon to create a light batter.

2 Lightly grease a hot griddle or large heavy-based frying pan (skillet) with lard. Drop on spoonfuls of the batter and cook for a few minutes until the tops of the pancakes are covered with bubbles and the undersides are golden brown. Flip them over and cook the other sides.

3 Remove the cooked pancakes from the griddle and wrap in a clean tea towel (dish cloth) while you cook the remainder.

4 Serve with butter, margarine or cream and jam.

🕐 **Preparation and cooking time:** 20 minutes

Prince Charlie's Pancakes

SERVES 4

	METRIC	IMPERIAL	AMERICAN
Plain (all-purpose) flour	100 g	4 oz	1 cup
A pinch of salt			
Eggs, beaten	2	2	2
Milk	300 ml	½ pt	1¼ cups
Lard (shortening)	25 g	1 oz	2 tbsp
Butter or margarine	75 g	3 oz	⅓ cup
Caster (superfine) sugar	100 g	4 oz	½ cup
Grated rind and juice of 3 large oranges			
Grated rind and juice of 2 large lemons			
Drambuie	30 ml	2 tbsp	2 tbsp

1 Sift the flour and salt into a bowl and make a well in the centre. Stir in the beaten eggs and half the milk and beat to a smooth batter, then gradually stir in the remaining milk.

2 Melt a little lard in a 20 cm/8 in frying pan (skillet). Pour in enough batter to cover the base of the pan, swirling the pan so that it is evenly coated, and fry (sauté) for a few minutes until bubbles appear on the surface. Turn the pancake over and cook the other side, then slide on to a tea towel (dish cloth) and keep warm. Make seven more pancakes in the same way.

3 Melt the butter or margarine in a frying pan, stir in the sugar and cook for 1 minute. Add the grated rind and juice of the oranges and lemons and bring to the boil. Add the Drambuie and simmer for 3 minutes.

4 Fold the pancakes into quarters and place in the frying pan. Cook gently for 3 minutes, spooning the sauce over the top, until heated through.

🕐 **Preparation and cooking time:** 15 minutes

Tipsy Lady Cake

SERVES 4

	METRIC	IMPERIAL	AMERICAN
Madeira or sherry	300 ml	½ pt	1¼ cups
Caster (superfine) sugar	115 g	2½ oz	good 1 cup
A squeeze of lemon juice			
Trifle sponges, split into halves	8	8	8
Greengage jam (conserve)	60 ml	4 tbsp	4 tbsp
Apricot jam, sieved (strained)	60 ml	4 tbsp	4 tbsp
Raspberry jam	60 ml	4 tbsp	4 tbsp
Egg whites	3	3	3
Blanched almonds, split	50 g	2 oz	½ cup
Lemon, thinly sliced	1	1	1
Single (light) cream	300 ml	½ pt	1¼ cups

1 Warm the Madeira or sherry and stir in 15 ml/1 tbsp of the sugar and the lemon juice.

2 Place four sponge cake halves in a shallow ovenproof dish and pour the wine mixture over them so that it soaks in evenly. Spread with greengage jam.

3 Place four more halves on top, soak with one-third of the wine mixture and spread with the apricot jam. Add another sponge layer, soak with more wine mixture and spread with the raspberry jam. Place the remaining sponge halves on top and soak with the remaining wine mixture.

4 Whisk the egg whites until stiff, then beat in the remaining sugar until thick and shiny. Spread over the layered cake and ruffle into small peaks. Sprinkle with the almonds.

5 Bake in a preheated oven at 180°C/350°F/gas mark 4 for about 20 minutes until the meringue is set.

6 Decorate the base of the meringue with the lemon slices and serve with cream.

⊘ **Preparation and cooking time:** 40 minutes

Curly Murly

If you use easy-blend dried yeast, halve the quantity and add to the flour and salt. Add the milk with the eggs.

SERVES 4

	METRIC	IMPERIAL	AMERICAN
Fresh yeast	*25 g*	*1 oz*	*2 tbsp*
Warm milk	*150 ml*	*¼ pt*	*⅔ cup*
Plain (all-purpose) flour	*350 g*	*12 oz*	*3 cups*
Salt	*1.5 ml*	*¼ tsp*	*¼ tsp*
Butter or margarine	*100 g*	*4 oz*	*½ cup*
Caster (superfine) sugar	*50 g*	*2 oz*	*¼ cup*
Grated rind and juice of *½ small lemon*			
Chopped mixed (candied) peel	*100 g*	*4 oz*	*⅔ cup*
Eggs, beaten	*2*	*2*	*2*
Melted butter or margarine	*30 ml*	*2 tbsp*	*2 tbsp*
Icing (confectioners') sugar	*100 g*	*4 oz*	*½ cup*
Chopped almonds	*25 g*	*1 oz*	*¼ cup*
Butter or margarine, to serve			

1 Dissolve the yeast in the warm milk.

2 Sift the flour and salt into a bowl, then rub in the butter or margarine. Stir in the sugar, lemon rind and mixed peel. Add the eggs and yeast liquid and beat well to a dough.

3 Knead the dough on a lightly floured board, then place in a large bowl, cover with a damp cloth and leave in a warm place for about 1 hour until doubled in size.

4 Divide the dough into three, knead each piece lightly and roll into 36 cm/14 in sausage shapes, then plait them together. Wet the ends and join them together to form a circle. Place on a baking (cookie) sheet, cover with oiled clingfilm (plastic wrap) and leave to prove for 20 minutes.

5 Brush with melted butter or margarine and bake in a preheated oven at 190°C/375°F/gas mark 5 for about 30 minutes until well risen and golden. Leave to cool.

6 Sift the icing sugar into a bowl and mix in 20 ml/ 1½ tbsp of the lemon juice. Trickle over the Curly Murly and sprinkle with chopped almonds. Serve sliced and buttered.

🕐 **Preparation and cooking time:** 2½ hours

Scottish Crumpets

MAKES ABOUT 10

	METRIC	IMPERIAL	AMERICAN
Caster (superfine) sugar	25 g	1 oz	2 tbsp
Egg	1	1	1
Milk	175 ml	6 fl oz	¾ cup
Plain (all-purpose) flour	100 g	4 oz	1 cup
A pinch of salt			
Cream of tartar	4 ml	¾ tsp	¾ tsp
Bicarbonate of soda			
(baking soda)	2.5 ml	½ tsp	½ tsp
Lard (shortening), for greasing			
Butter or margarine, to serve			

1 Put the sugar and egg in a bowl and whisk until thick and pale.

2 Stir in 150 ml/¼ pt/⅔ cup of the milk until well blended.

3 Sift the flour, salt and cream of tartar over the surface and gently whisk in until smooth.

4 Blend the bicarbonate of soda with the remaining milk and stir in.

5 Heat a greased griddle or heavy-based frying pan (skillet). Add large spoonfuls of the batter and cook until golden brown underneath and the surface is covered in burst bubbles.

6 Turn them over and cook the other sides. Transfer to a clean tea towel (dish cloth) while cooking the remainder. Serve warm with butter or margarine.

🕐 **Preparation and cooking time:** 20 minutes

Strawberry Sandwich

*Try this topped with halved strawberries. Glaze them with 30 ml/
2 tbsp warmed redcurrant or rowan jelly (clear conserve), blended
with 10 ml/2 tsp water, instead of the dusting of icing
(confectioners') sugar.*

SERVES 6–8

	METRIC	IMPERIAL	AMERICAN
Eggs, separated	*3*	*3*	*3*
Caster (superfine) sugar	*100 g*	*4 oz*	*½ cup*
Boiling water	*15 ml*	*1 tbsp*	*1 tbsp*
A few drops of vanilla essence (extract)			
Plain (all-purpose) flour	*75 g*	*3 oz*	*¾ cup*
Baking powder	*5 ml*	*1 tsp*	*1 tsp*
Double (heavy) cream	*150 ml*	*¼ pt*	*⅔ cup*
Strawberries	*100 g*	*4 oz*	*4 oz*
Icing sugar	*45 ml*	*3 tbsp*	*3 tbsp*

1 Grease and line the bases of two 20 cm/8 in sandwich
tins (pans) with non-stick baking parchment.

2 Using an electric beater, whisk the egg whites until stiff.
Whisk in the egg yolks one at a time, whisking well after each
addition until stiff. Whisk in the caster sugar, water and a few
drops of vanilla essence.

3 Sift the flour and baking powder over the surface and
fold in gently with a metal spoon.

4 Turn into the prepared tins and level the surfaces.
Bake in a preheated oven at 180°C/350°F/gas mark 4 for
20–25 minutes until risen, golden and the centres spring
back when lightly pressed.

5 Cool slightly, then turn out on to a wire rack, remove
the paper and leave to cool.

6 Whip the cream until peaking. Mash the strawberries
with 30 ml/2 tbsp of the icing sugar and a few drops of
vanilla essence. Use to sandwich the two cakes together.

⊕ **Preparation and cooking time:** 45 minutes

The West Coast

The leading city in this land of adventure and progress is Glasgow. Its go-ahead lifestyle and established industries have encouraged its many famous explorers, engineers and soldiers. With its taste for the future, it is hardly surprising that it pioneered the first tea shop and thus became the home of true baking. Baps (see page 66), Potato Scones (see page 63) and Paisley Almond Cakes (see page 69) all have their roots here.

But the west of Scotland is a land of surprising variety. You can be in the centre of a busy oil tanker depot and yet know that countless forest walks are but a short journey away. The beautiful Loch Lomond and the sands of Ayr and Girvin are favourites with holiday-makers whilst just a stone's throw inland is a thriving world of factories and farms.

In a place of such contrast, the easy-going people have developed a taste for unusual dishes. Mince Collops (see page 59) and Nettle Kale (see page 55) are firm favourites.

Cock-a-Leekie Soup

This was traditionally made with an old cockerel or boiling fowl, hence the name. In some parts of Scotland, cooks add 10 or 12 ready-to-eat prunes about 30 minutes before serving to give an unusual, sweet taste. If you prefer, you can reserve the meat to be served separately with Caper Sauce (see page 61).

SERVES 4–6

	METRIC	IMPERIAL	AMERICAN
Chicken with giblets, about 1.5 kg/3 lb	1	1	1
Water	2 litres	3½ pts	8½ cups
Salt	7.5 ml	1½ tsp	1½ tsp
Long-grain rice	30 ml	2 tbsp	2 tbsp
Leeks, sliced	6	6	6
Freshly ground black pepper			
Chopped fresh parsley	15 ml	1 tbsp	1 tbsp

1 Place the chicken and water in a large saucepan with the giblets and the salt. Bring to the boil, then reduce the heat, skim and simmer gently for 1½ hours.

2 Add the rice and leeks and cook for about a further 30 minutes until everything is tender. (If you use an old bird, cook until the legs pull off easily.) Remove the bird and the giblets, then skim the soup again and season to taste.

3 Chop the meat, discarding the skin and bones, and return to the soup. Serve sprinkled with chopped parsley.

⏱ **Preparation and cooking time:** 2½ hours

Nettle Kale

This is another dish that was traditionally made with a young cockerel or boiling fowl. The weight doesn't really matter – just cook until really tender.

SERVES 4

	METRIC	IMPERIAL	AMERICAN
Barley meal	75 g	3 oz	¾ cup
Butter or margarine, softened	50 g	2 oz	¼ cup
Garlic salt	5 ml	1 tsp	1 tsp
Freshly ground black pepper			
Chicken, about 1.5 kg/3 lb	1	1	1
Water	1.75 litres	3 pts	7½ cups
Onion, sliced	1	1	1
Tender nettles, finely chopped	350 g	12 oz	12 oz
Salt, to taste			
Fresh vegetables, to serve			

1 Make a stuffing for the bird by kneading 2 oz/50 g/ ½ cup of the barley meal into 25 g/1 oz/2 tbsp of the butter or margarine and seasoning with garlic salt and black pepper.

2 Push the stuffing into the chicken and tie the legs securely. Place in a large casserole dish (Dutch oven) or saucepan with the water.

3 Add the remaining barley meal, butter or margarine, onion and nettles, and season with salt and pepper. Bring to the boil, cover and simmer for 1½–2 hours until the chicken is very tender.

4 Serve the nettle broth first, then the chicken with fresh vegetables.

⏲ **Preparation and cooking time:** 2½ hours

Hotch Potch

This is essentially a summer soup, making the most of seasonal produce. Shredded cabbage is often used instead of the lettuce in winter. If preferred, the meat can be reserved and served separately.

SERVES 4

	METRIC	IMPERIAL	AMERICAN
Scrag end of lamb, trimmed of excess fat	900 g	2 lb	2 lb
Water	1.5 litres	2½ pts	6 cups
Salt and freshly ground black pepper			
Onion, chopped	1	1	1
Young carrots, diced	4	4	4
Large turnips, diced	3	3	3
Large potato, scrubbed and chopped	1	1	1
Shelled broad (fava) beans	175 g	6 oz	6 oz
Shelled peas	175 g	6 oz	6 oz
Small green cabbage, shredded	½	½	½
Small cauliflower, cut into florets	½	½	½
Chopped fresh mint	15 ml	1 tbsp	1 tbsp
Chopped fresh parsley	30 ml	2 tbsp	2 tbsp

1 Put the lamb in a large saucepan with the water, seasoning, onion, carrots and turnips.

2 Bring to the boil, skim the surface, reduce the heat, cover and simmer gently for 1½ hours.

3 Lift out the meat, remove the bones and discard. Cut into neat pieces and return to the pan.

4 Add all the remaining ingredients except the parsley and simmer for a further 30 minutes. Taste and adjust the seasoning.

5 Sprinkle with the parsley and serve.

⏲ **Preparation and cooking time:** 2 hours

Potted Hough

If you can't get hock of beef, use shin and ask your butcher for a beef bone to add flavour to the stock.

SERVES 4

	METRIC	IMPERIAL	AMERICAN
Hock of beef, cut into pieces	450 g	1 lb	1 lb
Knuckle of veal, cut into pieces	1 kg	2¼ lb	2¼ lb
Water	2 litres	3½ pts	8½ cups
Salt	5 ml	1 tsp	1 tsp
Whole pickling spices	2.5 ml	½ tsp	½ tsp
Black peppercorns	2.5 ml	½ tsp	½ tsp
Salad, to serve			

1 Place the meat, water and salt in a large saucepan, bring to the boil, then cover and simmer for 2–3 hours until the meat is really tender.

2 Remove the meat, discard the bones and mince (grind) the meat. Divide it between small ramekin dishes (custard cups).

3 Add the whole spices and peppercorns to the saucepan of cooking liquid. Simmer for a further 1½ hours. Strain the stock over the meat, leave to cool, then chill until set.

4 Serve cold with salad.

Preparation and cooking time: 4½ hours plus cooling and chilling

Ayrshire Galantine

*Traditionally this galantine would have been sewn into a pudding
cloth for boiling but it is much simpler to wrap it in foil!*

SERVES 4

	METRIC	IMPERIAL	AMERICAN
Ayrshire or other green			
back bacon	350 g	12 oz	12 oz
Braising steak	350 g	12 oz	12 oz
Fresh white breadcrumbs	150 g	6 oz	3 cups
Grated nutmeg	2.5 ml	½ tsp	½ tsp
Ground mace	1.5 ml	¼ tsp	¼ tsp
Salt and freshly ground black			
pepper			
Eggs, beaten	2	2	2
Stock or water	120 ml	4 fl oz	½ cup
Plain (all-purpose) flour	15 ml	1 tbsp	1 tbsp
Stock or water, for boiling			
Pickles, to serve			

1 Mince (grind) the two meats, then stir in the breadcrumbs and spices and season with salt and pepper. Stir in
the eggs and just enough stock or water to moisten.

2 Dust with flour and mould into a roll. Wrap tightly in a
double thickness of foil. Alternatively, press into a pudding
basin and cover with a double thickness of greased foil,
twisting under the rim to secure.

3 Half-fill a large pan with boiling stock or water, gently
add the galantine and simmer for 1½ hours.

4 Remove the galantine from the pan, place on a large
plate and cover with a second plate. Place some weights, or
cans of food, on top and leave to press overnight.

5 Remove from the foil, slice and serve with pickles.

🕘 **Preparation and cooking time:** 2½ hours

Mince Collops

A crushed garlic clove and a small handful of any fresh, chopped herbs will give this traditional dish a modern twist.

SERVES 4

	METRIC	IMPERIAL	AMERICAN
Minced (ground) steak	450 g	1 lb	1 lb
Shredded (chopped) suet	25 g	1 oz	¼ cup
Onion	1	1	1
Oatmeal	15 ml	1 tbsp	1 tbsp
Salt and freshly ground black pepper			
Beef stock	300 ml	½ pt	1¼ cups
Toast, poached eggs, grilled (broiled) tomatoes and bacon rolls, to serve			

1 Fry (sauté) the meat and suet in a frying pan (skillet) until browned. Add the whole onion, then stir in the oatmeal and season with salt and pepper. Pour in enough stock almost to cover the meat, bring to the boil, then simmer for 45–60 minutes. Discard the onion.

2 Serve spoonfuls of the collops on toast, topped with a poached egg and grilled tomatoes and bacon rolls.

🕐 **Preparation and cooking time:** 1½ hours

Mutton Pies

*Many Scottish recipes are traditionally made with mutton but lamb
is more readily available to the modern cook.*

SERVES 4

	METRIC	IMPERIAL	AMERICAN
Lean mutton or lamb, finely diced	350 g	12 oz	12 oz
Salt and freshly ground black pepper			
A pinch of grated nutmeg			
Plain (all-purpose) flour	450 g	1 lb	4 cups
Beef dripping, melted	100 g	4 oz	½ cup
Boiling water	300 ml	½ pt	1¼ cups
Mutton gravy or good stock	150 ml	¼ pt	⅔ cup
Egg, beaten	1	1	1

1 Season the meat with salt, pepper and nutmeg.

2 To make the pastry (paste), sift the flour and 2.5 ml/
½ tsp salt into a bowl. Pour in the melted dripping and the
boiling water and mix well with a wooden spoon to a dough.
Leave until cool enough to handle, then knead until smooth.

3 Reserve a quarter of the pastry, cover with a clean tea
towel (dish cloth) and keep it warm. Divide the rest into six
pieces, roll out on a lightly floured surface and use to line six
small pie tins (pans). Fill with the meat and moisten with a
little of the gravy or stock.

4 Cut six lids from the reserved pastry and press the
edges together. Make a hole in the centre of each top and
brush the tops with beaten egg.

5 Bake in a preheated oven at 350°F/180°C/gas mark 4
for 30 minutes.

6 Spoon a little more gravy into the pies and cook for a
further 10–15 minutes until golden. Serve immediately.

⏱ **Preparation and cooking time:** 1 hour

Caper Sauce

This sauce goes well with lamb and chicken recipes.

SERVES 4

	METRIC	IMPERIAL	AMERICAN
Butter or margarine	25 g	1 oz	2 tbsp
Plain (all-purpose) flour	25 g	1 oz	¼ cup
Milk	300 ml	½ pt	1¼ cups
Capers, chopped	15 ml	1 tbsp	1 tbsp
Vinegar from the jar of capers	15 ml	1 tbsp	1 tbsp
Salt and freshly ground black pepper			

1 Melt the butter or margarine in a small pan, then stir in the flour until blended and cook for 1 minute.

2 Remove from the heat and whisk in the milk, then return to the heat and bring slowly to the boil, stirring continuously.

3 Add the capers and vinegar and season to taste with salt and pepper. Simmer, stirring, for about 3 minutes until thick and smooth.

Preparation and cooking time: 10 minutes

Holiday Bacon

SERVES 4

	METRIC	IMPERIAL	AMERICAN
Bacon joint, soaked in cold water for several hours	2 kg	4½ lb	4½ lb
Water	1 litre	1¾ pts	4½ cups
Onion	1	1	1
Whole cloves	4	4	4
Chopped fresh parsley	15 ml	1 tbsp	1 tbsp
Dried thyme	2.5 ml	½ tsp	½ tsp
Dried rosemary	1.5 ml	¼ tsp	¼ tsp
Carrot, sliced	1	1	1
Black peppercorns	10	10	10
Light brown sugar	30 ml	2 tbsp	2 tbsp
Apple sauce, to serve			

1 Drain the bacon and place in a large, heavy saucepan with the water.

2 Stud the onion with the cloves and add it to the pan with the herbs, carrot and peppercorns. Cover and bring to the boil, then skim. Part-cover and simmer for 1½ hours.

3 Leave to stand until cool, then lift out the bacon and pull off the rind. Rub the sugar into the surface of the bacon and place it in a large roasting tin (pan), sugar-side up. Pour 30 ml/2 tbsp of the cooking liquor around and roast in a preheated oven at 200°C/400°F/gas mark 6 for 20 minutes or until lightly browned.

4 Serve with apple sauce.

⏱ **Preparation and cooking time:** 2 hours plus soaking and cooling

Potato Scones

SERVES 4

	METRIC	IMPERIAL	AMERICAN
Cooked potatoes	225 g	8 oz	8 oz
Butter or margarine, plus extra for spreading	15 g	½ oz	1 tbsp
Plain (all-purpose) flour	50 g	2 oz	½ cup
A large pinch of salt			
Lard (shortening), for greasing			

1 Mash the potatoes in a bowl with the butter or margarine, then beat in the flour and salt with a wooden spoon and continue to beat for a few minutes until very light.

2 Roll out very thinly on a lightly floured surface and cut into rounds with a 5 cm/2 in pastry (cookie) cutter.

3 Lightly grease a hot griddle or heavy-based frying pan (skillet) and cook the scones (biscuits) for a few minutes until browned on both sides.

4 Leave to cool and serve buttered.

⊙ **Preparation and cooking time:** 30 minutes

Sausage Skirlie-mirlie

SERVES 4

	METRIC	IMPERIAL	AMERICAN
Parsnips, cut into chunks	1 kg	2¼ lb	2¼ lb
Potatoes, cut into chunks	1 kg	2¼ lb	2¼ lb
Salt and freshly ground black pepper			
Sausages	450 g	1 lb	1 lb
Bacon fat, butter or margarine	50 g	2 oz	¼ cup
Hot milk (optional)	45 ml	3 tbsp	3 tbsp

1 Cook the parsnips and potatoes separately in boiling salted water until tender. Drain and mash, then mix together and season generously with salt and pepper.

2 Fry (sauté) the sausages in a little of the fat or butter or margarine until crisp, brown and cook through, then keep them warm. Pour the fat from the sausages into a saucepan, add the remaining bacon fat or butter or margarine and melt. Stir in the vegetables and beat over a medium heat until creamy, adding a little hot milk to make a lighter consistency, if liked.

3 Test and adjust the seasoning to taste, spoon the mashed vegetables into a warmed serving dish and arrange the sausages on top.

🕐 **Preparation and cooking time:** 40 minutes

Stovies

This dish can be made with just potatoes and onions, or you can add some chopped leftover meat 10–15 minutes before the end of the cooking time.

SERVES 4

	METRIC	IMPERIAL	AMERICAN
Good beef dripping	100 g	4 oz	½ cup
Onions, thinly sliced	4	4	4
Potatoes, thickly sliced	450 g	1 lb	1 lb
Salt and freshly ground black pepper			
Water	150 ml	¼ pt	⅔ cup

1 Melt the dripping in a heavy-based frying pan (skillet) and fry (sauté) the onions until beginning to soften.

2 Add the potatoes, season well with salt and pepper and add the water. Bring to the boil, then part-cover, reduce the heat and simmer gently for 1 hour, stirring occasionally, until the vegetables are tender. Serve hot.

🕐 **Preparation and cooking time:** 1¼ hours

Baps

Make sure that all the utensils, as well as the kitchen, are warm before starting to make bread, in order to get the best results. If you prefer to use easy-blend dried yeast, use half the given quantity. Simply add it to the flour, then work in the warm milk and water to make the dough.

MAKES 6

	METRIC	IMPERIAL	AMERICAN
Plain (all-purpose) flour, plus a little extra for dusting (optional)	225 g	8 oz	2 cups
Salt	5 ml	1 tsp	1 tsp
Lard (shortening)	25 g	1 oz	2 tbsp
Fresh yeast	15 g	½ oz	½ oz
Warm milk, plus a little extra for brushing	60 ml	4 tbsp	4 tbsp
Warm water	60 ml	4 tbsp	4 tbsp

1 Sift the flour and salt into a basin and rub in the lard.

2 Crumble the yeast into the warm milk and water and leave it to stand for about 15 minutes.

3 Gradually stir the yeast mixture into the flour and knead for about 10 minutes until smooth.

4 Place the dough in an oiled bowl, cover with oiled clingfilm (plastic wrap) and leave in a warm place for about 1 hour until the dough has doubled in size.

5 Turn on to a lightly floured surface and knead again thoroughly. Divide into six pieces and shape into flat oval rolls. Place on a greased baking (cookie) sheet, cover with the clingfilm again and leave in a warm place for a further 15 minutes.

6 Brush with milk and dust with flour, if liked, then bake in a preheated oven at 425°F/220°C/gas mark 7 for about 15 minutes until well risen and golden.

⊙ **Preparation and cooking time:** 55 minutes plus rising

Rothesay Pudding

SERVES 4

	METRIC	IMPERIAL	AMERICAN
Self-raising (self-rising) flour	100 g	4 oz	1 cup
Fresh white breadcrumbs	100 g	4 oz	2 cups
Shredded (chopped) suet	100 g	4 oz	1 cup
Caster (superfine) sugar	15 ml	1 tbsp	1 tbsp
Egg, lightly beaten	1	1	1
Raspberry or gooseberry jam			
(conserve)	275 g	10 oz	good ¾ cup
Milk	250 ml	8 fl oz	1 cup
Bicarbonate of soda			
(baking soda)	5 ml	1 tsp	1 tsp
Distilled vinegar	2.5 ml	½ tsp	½ tsp
Cream or custard, to serve			

1 Mix together all the ingredients except the bicarbonate of soda and the vinegar. Blend these two together, then mix them into all the other ingredients.

2 Transfer the mixture to a greased 1 litre/1¾ pt/4½ cup pudding basin and cover with a double thickness of pleated greaseproof (waxed) paper, twisting and folding under the rim to secure. Place the basin in a large saucepan and fill with enough boiling water to come halfway up the sides of the basin.

3 Cover and steam for 2 hours, topping up with boiling water as necessary.

4 Turn out and serve with cream or custard.

🕑 **Preparation and cooking time:** 2½ hours

Helensburgh Toffee

This toffee has the consistency of thick fudge when ready.

MAKES ABOUT 700 G/1½ LB

	METRIC	IMPERIAL	AMERICAN
Unsalted (sweet) butter	50 g	2 oz	¼ cup
Caster (superfine) sugar	450 g	1 lb	2 cups
Golden (light corn) syrup	10 ml	2 tsp	2 tsp
Can of condensed milk	200 ml	7 fl oz	1 small
Milk	60 ml	4 tbsp	4 tbsp
Vanilla essence (extract)	2.5 ml	½ tsp	½ tsp

1 Melt the butter in a heavy-based saucepan, then add the sugar, syrup, condensed milk and milk. Heat very gently until dissolved, then bring to the boil, stirring all the time. Continue to heat, still stirring gently, to 115°C/242°F on a sugar thermometer, or until a teaspoonful of the mixture forms a soft ball when dropped into cold water.

2 Remove from the heat, then add the vanilla essence and beat well until thick and creamy. Pour into greased tins (pans) and mark into squares, then leave to cool and set.

3 Cut into pieces and store in an airtight container.

⊕ **Preparation and cooking time:** 40 minutes

Paisley Almond Cakes

MAKES 12

	METRIC	IMPERIAL	AMERICAN
Cornflour (cornstarch)	50 g	2 oz	½ cup
Rice flour	50 g	2 oz	½ cup
Baking powder	5 ml	1 tsp	1 tsp
Butter or margarine	75 g	3 oz	⅓ cup
Caster (superfine) sugar	75 g	3 oz	⅓ cup
Eggs, beaten	2	2	2
Ground almonds	30 ml	2 tbsp	2 tbsp
Blanched almonds, halved	6	6	6

1 Sift together the flours and baking powder. Cream together the butter or margarine and sugar.

2 Gradually stir in a spoonful of the flours and baking powder, then a spoonful of beaten egg and beat well. Continue adding all the remaining flours and eggs in alternate spoonfuls and beat until the mixture is white and creamy.

3 Gently fold in the ground almonds.

4 Spoon into greased and floured bun tins (patty pans), top each with a sliced almond and bake in a preheated oven at 180°C/350°F/gas mark 4 for about 15 minutes until risen, golden and firm to the touch. Transfer to a wire rack to cool.

⏲ **Preparation and cooking time:** 25 minutes

The Islands

Around the coast of Scotland there are uncounted islands. Some are large and some are small, some thrive under industrial progress, and others are inhabited only by flora and fauna.

The Islanders have, through the ages, become experts in self-sufficiency. The poor soil is carefully tended to yield the widest variety of food, and crofting is still very much a way of life. A substantial dish like Carageen Pudding (see page 77) can, it seems, be made from next to nothing – and every last piece of meat is used to its fullest advantage.

Life on the Islands can be extremely tough and there is little place for fancy ideals and extravagant foods. This section contains down-to-earth, no-nonsense meals, perfect for keeping the family warm, healthy and happy.

Potato Soup

Try using leeks instead of onions, and substitute chicken or any meat stock for the water.

SERVES 4

	METRIC	IMPERIAL	AMERICAN
Potatoes, diced	6	6	6
Onions, chopped	3	3	3
Water	750 ml	1¼ pts	3 cups
Salt and freshly ground black pepper			
Butter or margarine	25 g	1 oz	2 tbsp
Cheddar cheese, grated	50 g	2 oz	½ cup

1 Boil the potatoes and onions in the water for about 15 minutes until the potatoes disintegrate.

2 Season to taste with salt and pepper, work in the butter or margarine and serve with a sprinkling of grated cheese.

🕐 **Preparation and cooking time:** 30 minutes

Orkney Cheese

This traditional cheese would originally have been made with a gallon of milk (4.5 litres). This baby version is more manageable and fun to make and will give you a real taste of the Scottish Isles. It uses vegetarian rennet, but you can use animal rennet if you prefer. You will need to double the quantity. Also, make sure that you scald your disposable cloths and all bowls and utensils by plunging them into boiling water before use. Finally, try ringing the changes by flavouring the curds with a small crushed garlic clove and 15 ml/1 tbsp snipped fresh chives or chopped fresh mixed herbs before pressing.

MAKES 1 SMALL CHEESE

	METRIC	IMPERIAL	AMERICAN
Full cream milk	1.2 litres	2 pts	5 cups
Vegetarian rennet	2.5 ml	½ tsp	½ tsp
Cold, previously boiled, water	15 ml	1 tbsp	1 tbsp
Salt			

1 Warm the milk to blood temperature, when it feels neither hot nor cold.

2 Mix the rennet with the water and stir thoroughly into the milk. Tip into a bowl and leave to stand until set.

3 Cut through the curds haphazardly with a knife and chill for a further 15 minutes.

4 Lay a scalded disposable cloth in a sieve (strainer) over a bowl. Tip in the curds and whey. Draw the ends of the cloth over the surface and leave to drip in the fridge for 24 hours.

5 Line a 10–12.5 cm/4–5 in diameter dish with a clean, scalded disposable cloth. Stand the dish on a plate, scrape in the strained curds and cover with the cloth ends.

6 Place a small saucer that fits inside the rim on the top of the dish and weight down with heavy weights.

7 Return to the fridge. Every 24 hours, remove the cheese and unwrap. Line the dish with a clean cloth, turn the cheese over, return to the dish, cover and weigh down again.

8 After 8 days, unwrap the cheese from the cloth and serve. Store any unused cheese in the fridge, wrapped in clingfilm (plastic wrap).

🕐 **Preparation time:** 15 minutes plus standing

Lambs' Liver Pâté

SERVES 4

	METRIC	IMPERIAL	AMERICAN
Butter or margarine	*175 g*	*6 oz*	*¾ cup*
Lambs' liver, finely chopped	*225 g*	*8 oz*	*8 oz*
Streaky bacon rashers (slices), rinded and chopped	*175 g*	*6 oz*	*6 oz*
Onion, chopped	*1*	*1*	*1*
Garlic clove, chopped	*1*	*1*	*1*
Bay leaf	*1*	*1*	*1*
Sherry	*60 ml*	*4 tbsp*	*4 tbsp*
Salt and freshly ground black pepper			

1 Melt all but 25g/1 oz/2 tbsp of the butter or margarine in a frying pan (skillet) and gently fry (sauté) the liver, bacon, onion, garlic and bay leaf for 15 minutes.

2 Remove the bay leaf, then mince (grind) the mixture finely or purée in a blender or food processor.

3 Add the sherry and salt and pepper to taste and beat well. Spoon into a small pâté dish.

4 Melt the remaining butter or margarine and pour over the top to seal the surface. Leave until cold, then chill and eat within 24 hours.

🕐 **Preparation and cooking time:** 30 minutes plus chilling

Arran Potato Salad

The Island cook would use Arran Chief potatoes for this recipe but you can use any waxy variety. If you prefer, use mayonnaise instead of salad dressing or cream and sharpen slightly with white wine vinegar.

SERVES 4

	METRIC	IMPERIAL	AMERICAN
Waxy potatoes, diced	10	10	10
Shelled fresh or frozen peas	100 g	4 oz	4 oz
Cooked beetroot (red beets), diced	100 g	4 oz	4 oz
Salt and freshly ground black pepper			
Chopped fresh parsley	5 ml	1 tsp	1 tsp
Chopped onion	10 ml	2 tsp	2 tsp
Salad dressing or salad cream	60 ml	4 tbsp	4 tbsp
Sprigs of fresh parsley, to garnish			

1 Cook the potatoes in boiling salted water for 10 minutes or until tender, then drain and pat dry.

2 Cook the peas separately for about 5 minutes until tender, then drain.

3 Mix together all the vegetables while still warm, then stir in the parsley and onion and season to taste with salt and pepper.

4 Carefully fold in the salad dressing or salad cream to moisten and garnish with fresh parsley.

⏲ **Preparation and cooking time:** 20 minutes

Clapshot

Ideal to accompany stews or other meat dishes, this is a traditional combination of potatoes and turnips.

SERVES 4

	METRIC	IMPERIAL	AMERICAN
Potatoes, cut into chunks	*450 g*	*1 lb*	*1 lb*
Turnips, cut into chunks	*450 g*	*1 lb*	*1 lb*
Beef dripping, butter or margarine	*25 ml*	*1 oz*	*2 tbsp*
Small onion, chopped	*1*	*1*	*1*
Salt and freshly ground black pepper			
Snipped fresh chives	*15 ml*	*1 tbsp*	*1 tbsp*
A knob of butter or margarine			
A sprig of parsley, to garnish			

1 Boil the potatoes and turnips for about 15 minutes until tender, then drain and return to the pan. Stir over a gentle heat for about a minute until dry. Mash the vegetables together.

2 Melt the dripping, butter or margarine in a frying pan (skillet) and fry (sauté) the onion gently for 3 minutes until softened but not browned.

3 Stir the onion into the vegetables and season generously with salt and pepper. Stir in the chives.

4 Stir in a knob of butter or margarine and garnish with the parsley.

🕐 **Preparation and cooking time:** 25 minutes

Cheese Charlotte

If you cannot buy Scottish cheese, use any strongly flavoured Cheddar or other hard variety.

SERVES 4

	METRIC	IMPERIAL	AMERICAN
Fresh white breadcrumbs	30 ml	2 tbsp	2 tbsp
Slices of white bread, crusts removed	6	6	6
Butter or margarine	50 g	2 oz	¼ cup
Scottish Cheddar cheese, grated	150 g	6 oz	1½ cups
Salt and freshly ground black pepper			
Eggs	2	2	2
Milk	375 ml	13 fl oz	1½ cups
Piece of cucumber, sliced	5 cm	2 in	2 in
Tomatoes, sliced	2	2	2
Green salad, to serve			

1 Grease a charlotte mould or 18 cm/7 in soufflé dish and sprinkle with the breadcrumbs. Spread the bread with the butter or margarine and layer with the cheese, salt and pepper in the prepared container, ending with a layer of cheese.

2 Beat together the eggs and milk, then gradually pour into the mould and leave for 10 minutes for the liquid to be absorbed.

3 Bake in a preheated oven at 190°C/375°F/gas mark 5 for 20–30 minutes until set.

4 Leave to cool, then turn out and garnish with cucumber and tomatoes. Serve with a green salad.

🕐 **Preparation and cooking time:** 40 minutes plus cooling

Carageen Pudding

Carageen is a type of sea moss. You should be able to find it in packets at specialist food shops and some supermarkets. This pudding is also good flavoured with other citrus rind or a little vanilla essence (extract).

SERVES 4

	METRIC	IMPERIAL	AMERICAN
Dried carageen	15 g	½ oz	1 tbsp
Milk	600 ml	1 pt	2½ cups
Grated rind and juice of 1 lemon			
Caster (superfine) sugar	25 g	1 oz	2 tbsp
A pinch of salt			
Single (light) cream, to serve			

1 Put the carageen in a bowl with just enough cold water to cover and leave to soak for 10 minutes, then drain.

2 Warm the milk with the lemon rind and juice and the sugar, then add the carageen. Bring to the boil, reduce the heat and simmer gently for about 20 minutes until soft and thick. It should set to a jelly when tested on a cold plate.

3 Strain into a rinsed 600 ml/1 pt/2½ cup china or glass mould and leave in a cool place to set.

4 Turn out and serve with cream.

⊘ **Preparation and cooking time:** 30 minutes plus setting

Urney Pudding

This pudding tastes even better served with a sauce made from a strawbery jelly tablet, dissolved in 150 ml/¼ pt/⅔ cup boiling water.

SERVES 6

	METRIC	IMPERIAL	AMERICAN
Butter or margarine, softened	100 g	4 oz	½ cup
Strawberry jam (conserve)	225 g	8 oz	⅔ cup
Eggs	2	2	2
Self-raising (self-rising) flour	100 g	4 oz	1 cup
Bicarbonate of soda			
(baking soda)	2.5 ml	½ tsp	½ tsp
Milk	15 ml	1 tbsp	1 tbsp
Pouring cream, to serve			

1 Put the butter or margarine, jam and eggs in a bowl. Sift the flour over the surface and beat all together until smooth.

2 Mix the bicarbonate of soda with the milk and stir in.

3 Turn into a greased 900 ml/1½ pt/3¾ cup pudding basin. Cover with a double thickness of greased greaseproof (waxed) paper, twisting and folding under the rim to secure.

4 Steam for 2 hours. Turn out and serve with the cream.

🕐 **Preparation and cooking time:** 2¼ hours

Islay Loaf

MAKES ONE 20 CM/8 IN CAKE

	METRIC	IMPERIAL	AMERICAN
Raisins	175 g	6 oz	1 cup
Light brown sugar	175 g	6 oz	¾ cup
Cold water	300 ml	½ pt	1¼ cups
Golden (light corn) syrup	15 ml	1 tbsp	1 tbsp
Butter or margarine	15 g	½ oz	1 tbsp
Self-raising (self-rising) flour	275 g	10 oz	2½ cups
Bicarbonate of soda (baking soda)	10 ml	2 tsp	2 tsp
Mixed (apple-pie) spice	10 ml	2 tsp	2 tsp
Walnuts, chopped	50 g	2 oz	½ cup

1 Warm the raisins, sugar, water, syrup and butter or margarine in a saucepan until the fat has melted. Allow to cool slightly.

2 Fold in the flour, bicarbonate of soda, spice and walnuts.

3 Spoon into a greased and lined 20 cm/8 in cake tin (pan) and bake in a preheated oven at 180°C/350°F/gas mark 4 for 1 hour until a skewer inserted in the centre comes out clean.

4 Turn out on to a wire rack, remove the paper and leave to cool.

🕐 **Preparation and cooking time:** 1¼ hours

Broonie

Use plain yoghurt instead of buttermilk if you prefer.

MAKES 9 SQUARES

	METRIC	IMPERIAL	AMERICAN
Plain (all-purpose) flour	100 g	4 oz	1 cup
Medium oatmeal	100 g	4 oz	1 cup
Light brown sugar	75 g	3 oz	⅓ cup
Butter or margarine	50 g	2 oz	¼ cup
Ground ginger	10 ml	2 tsp	2 tsp
Bicarbonate of soda (baking soda)	7.5 ml	1½ tsp	1½ tsp
Black treacle (molasses)	30 ml	2 tbsp	2 tbsp
Egg, lightly beaten	1	1	1
Buttermilk	150 ml	¼ pt	⅔ cup

1 Sift the flour into a bowl and stir in the oatmeal and sugar. Rub in the butter or margarine, then stir in the ginger and bicarbonate of soda.

2 Mix the treacle with the egg and buttermilk and beat into the mixture to form a thick batter.

3 Pour into a greased and lined 18 cm/7 in square baking tin (pan) and bake in the centre of a preheated oven at 160°C/325°F/gas mark 3 for 50 minutes until firm and a skewer inserted into the centre comes out clean.

4 Turn out, remove the paper and leave to cool on a wire rack. Serve cut into squares.

🕐 **Preparation and cooking time:** 1¼ hours

The East Coast and Central Lowlands

Bygone kings and queens vied for fame and beautiful castles and palaces abound in this area, the home of Scottish culture. Mary Queen of Scots, for one, is associated with nearly every historic castle from Falkland to Tantallon. Her life at Holyrood in Edinburgh makes a colourful chapter in any history book, a thrilling mixture of romance, mystery and murder.

This part of the country is a sportsman's dream, for Eastern Scotland boasts the greatest golf courses in Britain, if not in Europe, such as Gleneagles in Perthshire and the Royal and Ancient at St Andrews. Fife alone has over 30 courses.

With this awe-inspiring heritage reflected in local fare, some very distinctive dishes have resulted. Forfar Bridies (see page 88) and Kingdom of Fife Pie (see page 84) are amongst the tastiest meat pies in the world, and Poached Arbroath Smokies (see page 85) are a must for every visitor.

Mussel Brose

*For a richer soup, use half milk and half buttermilk and add 15 ml/
1 tbsp Scotch whisky just before serving.*

SERVES 4

	METRIC	IMPERIAL	AMERICAN
Mussels	1.75 kg	4 lb	4 lb
Water	300 ml	½ pt	1¼ cups
Fine oatmeal	30 ml	2 tbsp	2 tbsp
Milk	600 ml	1 pt	2½ cups
Small onion, finely chopped	1	1	1
Butter or margarine	15 g	½ oz	1 tbsp
Salt and freshly ground black pepper			
Chopped fresh parsley	30 ml	2 tbsp	2 tbsp

1 Scrub the mussels and remove the beards. Discard any
that are open or don't close when sharply tapped. Place in a
large saucepan with the water. Cover and bring to the boil,
reduce the heat and cook for 5 minutes, shaking the pan
occasionally. Discard any that remain closed.

2 Strain the cooking liquid into a bowl. Remove the
mussels from their shells, and add to the liquor.

3 Lightly toast the oatmeal in a dry saucepan until
golden. Add the milk, bring to the boil and simmer for
5 minutes, stirring.

4 Fry (sauté) the onion in the butter or margarine in the
rinsed-out mussel saucepan. Add the mussels in their liquor
and bring to the boil.

5 Stir in the oatmeal milk, season to taste and serve
sprinkled with the parsley.

⏱ **Preparation and cooking time:** 45 minutes

Forth Lobster

SERVES 2

	METRIC	IMPERIAL	AMERICAN
Cooked lobster about 1 kg/2¼ lb	1	1	1
Butter or margarine	75 g	3 oz	⅓ cup
Plain (all-purpose) flour	25 g	1 oz	¼ cup
Milk	300 ml	½ pt	1¼ cups
Egg yolks	2	2	2
Single (light) cream	150 ml	¼ pt	⅔ cup
Salt and freshly ground black pepper			
Drambuie	30 ml	2 tbsp	2 tbsp
Chopped fresh parsley	15 ml	1 tbsp	1 tbsp

1 Twist the claws off the lobster and crack them open. Remove the meat, chop and set aside. Halve the lobster lengthways and remove the gills, stomach sac and the black intestine that runs down the length of the body. Scoop out the meat and any coral or green creamy liver. Rinse the shells and keep warm.

2 Melt 25 g/1 oz/2 tbsp of the butter or margarine in a saucepan and stir in the flour. Remove from the heat and whisk in the milk, then return to the heat and whisk until smooth.

3 Blend the egg yolks with the cream, add to the sauce and season to taste. Keep warm but do not allow the sauce to boil or it will curdle.

4 Melt the remaining butter or margarine in a frying pan (skillet), toss in the lobster meat and add the Drambuie. Mix in the sauce and parsley. Scoop back into the lobster shells and serve hot.

🕐 **Preparation and cooking time:** 30 minutes

Kingdom of Fife Pie

Traditionally, a fresh rabbit would have been used for this recipe, skinned, jointed and then soaked for 30 minutes before cooking. Stock would have been made from the head, giblets and bones. If you do not wish to make your own rough puff pastry (paste), use bought puff pastry instead.

SERVES 4

	METRIC	IMPERIAL	AMERICAN
Rabbit portions	4	4	4
Pickled salt pork, sliced	350 g	12 oz	12 oz
Grated nutmeg	5 ml	1 tsp	1 tsp
Salt and freshly ground black pepper			
Hard-boiled (hard-cooked) eggs, quartered	2	2	2
Fresh breadcrumbs	60 ml	4 tbsp	4 tbsp
Bacon rashers (slices), rinded and chopped	2	2	2
Dried mixed herbs	5 ml	1 tsp	1 tsp
Chopped fresh parsley	5 ml	1 tsp	1 tsp
Egg, beaten	1	1	1
White wine (optional)	45 ml	3 tbsp	3 tbsp
Rabbit or chicken stock	300 ml	½ pt	1¼ cups
Rough puff pastry	225 g	8 oz	8 oz
A little milk, to glaze			

1 Arrange the rabbit joints and sliced pork in a large, deep pie dish and season with nutmeg, salt and pepper. Add the hard-boiled eggs to the dish.

2 Mix together the breadcrumbs, bacon, herbs and parsley and season to taste with salt and pepper. Bind with the beaten egg and roll into little balls. Place in the pie dish.

3 Pour the wine over the meat, if using, and add enough stock to fill the dish two-thirds full.

4 Roll out the pastry on a lightly floured surface and use to cover the pie. Make three holes in the pastry to allow steam to escape. Brush with milk to glaze.

5 Bake in a preheated oven at 220°C/425°F/gas mark 7 for 15 minutes, then reduce the oven temperature to 160°C/325°F/gas mark 3 for a further 1½–2 hours, covering with greaseproof (waxed) paper to prevent over-browning.

🕐 **Preparation and cooking time:** 2½ hours

Poached Arbroath Smokies

This cooking method can be used just as successfully with other smoked fish such as mackerel.

SERVES 4

	METRIC	IMPERIAL	AMERICAN
Water	*150 ml*	*¼ pt*	*⅔ cup*
Arbroath smokies	*4*	*4*	*4*
Unsalted (sweet) butter	*50 g*	*2 oz*	*¼ cup*
Lemon, sliced	*1*	*1*	*1*

1 Pour water into a frying pan (skillet) so that it is 1 cm/½ in deep and bring to the boil. Slide the fish into the pan, cover and cook for a few minutes until heated through. Drain well.

2 Serve the fish with knobs of butter and slices of lemon.

🕐 **Preparation and cooking time:** 10 minutes

Musselburgh Pie

Home-made rough puff pastry (paste) is traditional for this pie, but it is easier to use bought puff pastry.

SERVES 4

	METRIC	IMPERIAL	AMERICAN
Minute steak	450 g	1 lb	1 lb
Oysters, shelled	12	12	12
Bacon fat or lard (shortening)	50 g	2 oz	¼ cup
Shallot, sliced	1	1	1
Plain (all-purpose) flour	25 g	1 oz	¼ cup
Salt and freshly ground black pepper			
Chicken or vegetable stock	175 ml	6 fl oz	¾ cup
Puff pastry	225 g	8 oz	8 oz
Egg, beaten	1	1	1

1 Beat the steak flat, then cut into strips as wide as the oysters.

2 Halve the oysters and dot each half with bacon fat or lard. Place a slice of shallot between the oyster halves, sandwich them together and wrap in a strip of the meat.

3 Sift the flour into a small bowl and season with salt and pepper. Dip each meat roll in the flour, then pack into a pie dish. Place a pie funnel or upturned eggcup in the centre and add the stock.

4 Roll out the pastry on a lightly floured surface and use to cover the pie. Trim and flute the edges, then brush with beaten egg.

5 Cook in a preheated oven at 200°C/400°F/gas mark 6 for 15 minutes, then reduce the oven temperature to 180°C/350°F/gas mark 4 and bake for a further 1¼ hours until the pastry is golden and the meat rolls are cooked. Cover lightly with greaseproof (waxed) paper or foil if it starts to brown too quickly.

🕐 **Preparation and cooking time:** 2 hours

Wild Duck with Port

Wild duck was traditionally used for this recipe, hung until a greenish tinge appeared around the belly! However, you can use small, oven-ready duckling instead.

SERVES 4

	METRIC	IMPEIAL	AMERICAN
Oven-ready duckling	2	2	2
Streaky bacon rashers (slices), rinded	6	6	6
Butter or margarine	25 g	1 oz	2 tbsp
Cayenne	5 ml	1 tsp	1 tsp
Salt and freshly ground black pepper			
Port	120 ml	4 fl oz	½ cup
Juice of 1 lemon			
Mushroom ketchup (catsup)	15 ml	1 tbsp	1 tbsp
Orange marmalade	30 ml	2 tbsp	2 tbsp
Brandy, warmed	30 ml	2 tbsp	2 tbsp

1 Cover the ducks' breasts with the bacon and place in a large roasting tin (pan) with the butter or margarine. Roast in a preheated oven for 1 hour at 180°C/350°F/gas mark 4 until the ducks are tender.

2 Remove the bacon and score the breasts two or three times, then sprinkle with cayenne, salt and pepper.

3 Pour over the port and the lemon juice and return to the oven for 5 minutes. Transfer the ducks to a warmed serving dish and keep them warm while making the sauce.

4 Skim off any fat, then add the mushroom ketchup and marmalade to the pan juices and cook over a gentle heat, adding a little water if necessary, to make a smooth gravy. Strain into a sauceboat.

5 At the table, pour the brandy over the birds and ignite. Carve or cut the birds in half. Serve the gravy separately.

⏱ **Preparation and cooking time:** 1¼ hours

Forfar Bridies

*Traditionally the pastry (paste) is made of only flour, salt and water,
but this makes a rather tough casing. Many Scots cooks nowadays
prefer to use shortcrust (basic pie crust) or suet pastry while others
use rough puff or flaky pastry. In some parts of Scotland, the filling
is placed in the centre of the pastry and the edges brought over the
top before being sealed and notched. If you use this method, prick
the bridies well with a fork instead of making a hole in the centre.*

SERVES 4

	METRIC	IMPERIAL	AMERICAN
Topside or rump steak	*450 g*	*1 lb*	*1 lb*
Shortcrust pastry	*450 g*	*1 lb*	*1 lb*
Shredded (chopped) suet	*75 g*	*3 oz*	*¾ cup*
Onion, finely chopped	*30 ml*	*2 tbsp*	*2 tbsp*
Salt and freshly ground black pepper			

1 Beat the meat well with a rolling pin, then cut into
narrow strips 2.5 cm/1 in long.

2 Divide the pastry into three or four rounds and spread
the meat strips over half of each round. Add a layer of suet
followed by a layer of onion and season well. Dampen the
edges, fold in half and seal and flute the edges together. Make
a hole in the top to allow the steam to escape.

3 Place on a greased baking (cookie) sheet and bake in a
preheated oven at 230°C/450°F/gas mark 8 for 15 minutes,
then reduce the oven temperature to 180°C/350°F/gas
mark 4 and bake for a further 1 hour until the meat feels
tender when tested with a skewer. Cover loosely with
greaseproof (waxed) paper or foil if over-browning. Serve hot.

🕐 **Preparation and cooking time:** 1½ hours

Dunfillan Pudding

You can use any stewed fruit or jam (conserve) instead of the apple and blackberry mixture.

SERVES 4

	METRIC	IMPERIAL	AMERICAN
Cooking (tart) apple, sliced	1	1	1
Ripe blackberries	50 g	2 oz	2 oz
Caster (superfine) sugar	40 g	1½ oz	3 tbsp
Plain (all-purpose) flour	50 g	2 oz	½ cup
A pinch of salt			
Milk	300 ml	½ pt	1¼ cups
Butter or margarine, plus a little for greasing	25 g	1 oz	2 tbsp
A few drops of vanilla essence (extract)			
Eggs	2	2	2

1 Put the apple slices and blackberries in a saucepan with 15 g/½ oz/1 tbsp of the sugar. Cover and cook, stirring occasionally, for about 5 minutes until soft.

2 Turn into a lightly greased 1.2 litre/2 pt/5 cup ovenproof dish and spread out evenly.

3 Blend the flour and salt with the remaining sugar and a little of the milk in a saucepan. Blend in the remaining milk and add the butter or margarine. Bring to the boil, stirring until thick and smooth.

4 Cool slightly, then beat in the vanilla essence and eggs. Pour over the fruit and bake in a preheated oven at 180°C/350°F/gas mark 4 for about 20 minutes until golden and set. Serve while still hot.

⏲ **Preparation and cooking time:** 35 minutes

Crail Pudding

SERVES 4

	METRIC	IMPERIAL	AMERICAN
Butter or margarine	50 g	2 oz	¼ cup
Plain (all-purpose) flour	50 g	2 oz	½ cup
Milk	600 ml	1 pt	2½ cups
Caster (superfine) sugar	25 g	1 oz	2 tbsp
Vanilla essence (extract)	5 ml	1 tsp	1 tsp
Eggs, separated	2	2	2
Ground cinnamon or grated nutmeg, to decorate			

1 Melt the butter or margarine in a saucepan, then stir in the flour and cook for 2 minutes. Remove from the heat and whisk in the milk gradually until smooth. Return to the heat and stir until boiling, then reduce the heat and simmer for 5 minutes.

2 Add the sugar, vanilla essence and egg yolks.

3 Whisk the egg whites until stiff, then fold into the mixture.

4 Pour into a greased pie dish and bake at 180°C/350°F/gas mark 4 for 30 minutes. Serve hot, sprinkled with cinnamon or nutmeg.

⊙ **Preparation and cooking time:** 40 minutes

Cranachan

SERVES 4

	METRIC	IMPERIAL	AMERICAN
Medium oatmeal	50 g	2 oz	½ cup
Double (heavy) cream	300 ml	½ pt	1¼ cups
Icing (confectioners') sugar	45 ml	3 tbsp	3 tbsp
Raspberries	225 g	8 oz	8 oz
Sprigs of mint, to decorate (optional)			

1 Toast the oatmeal in a heavy-based frying pan (skillet) until lightly browned. Tip on to a plate.

2 Whip the cream with the sugar until peaking. Fold in the oatmeal.

3 Layer the cream mixture with the raspberries in win goblets, finishing with a layer of raspberries. Decorate with sprigs of mint, if liked.

🕐 **Preparation time:** 10 minutes

Barley Pudding

SERVES 4

	METRIC	IMPERIAL	AMERICAN
Barley	*225 g*	*8 oz*	*good 1 cup*
Water	*1 litre*	*1¾ pts*	*4¼ cups*
Currants	*75 g*	*3 oz*	*⅓ cup*
Raisins	*50 g*	*2 oz*	*⅓ cup*

A pinch of salt
Caster (superfine) sugar and
single (light) cream, to serve

1 Place the barley and water in a heavy-based saucepan. Bring slowly to the boil, then simmer for 1½ hours, stirring occasionally.

2 Add the currants and raisins to the barley with the salt and simmer for a further 15 minutes, stirring occasionally.

3 Sprinkle with caster sugar and serve with single cream.

🕐 **Preparation and cooking time:** 1¾ hours

Holyrood Pudding

SERVES 4

	METRIC	IMPERIAL	AMERICAN
Milk	600 ml	1 pt	2½ cups
Caster (superfine) sugar	75 g	3 oz	⅓ cup
Semolina (cream of wheat)	65 g	2½ oz	⅓ cup
Ratafia biscuits (cookies), crushed	50 g	2 oz	2 oz
Butter or margarine	25 g	1 oz	2 tbsp
Eggs, separated	3	3	3
Orange marmalade	15 ml	1 tbsp	1 tbsp
For the sauce:			
Egg	1	1	1
Caster (superfine) sugar	25 g	1 oz	2 tbsp
Milk	120 ml	¼ pt	⅔ cup
Ground almonds	25 g	1 oz	¼ cup
Orange flower water	15 ml	1 tbsp	1 tbsp

1 To make the pudding, bring the milk to the boil in a saucepan and stir in the sugar, semolina, crushed biscuits and butter or margarine. Simmer for 5 minutes, stirring constantly, then pour into a bowl and leave to cool.

2 Beat in the egg yolks, one at a time, then add the marmalade. Whisk the egg whites until stiff, then carefully fold them into the mixture.

3 Spoon the mixture into a greased 900 ml/1½ pt/3¾ cup pudding basin and cover with greased and pleated greaseproof (waxed) paper, twisting and folding under the rim to secure. Place in a large saucepan and fill with enough boiling water to come halfway up the sides of the basin. Cover and steam for 1¼ hours, topping up with boiling water as necessary.

4 Meanwhile, whisk all the sauce ingredients together. Heat in the top of a double boiler for about 10 minutes, stirring continuously, until thick.

5 Turn out the pudding and serve with the sauce.

🕙 **Preparation and cooking time:** 1½ hours

St Fillan's Paste

If you are using prunes or figs for this dish, you may need to add a little apple juice to moisten the fruit or the pudding will be too dry.

SERVES 4

	METRIC	IMPERIAL	AMERICAN
Plain (all-purpose) flour	100 g	4 oz	1 cup
Caster (superfine) sugar	50 g	2 oz	¼ cup
Cream of tartar	2.5 ml	½ tsp	½ tsp
Bicarbonate of soda (baking soda)	1.5 ml	¼ tsp	¼ tsp
A pinch of salt			
Butter or margarine, plus extra for greasing	40 g	1½ oz	3 tbsp
Eggs	2	2	2
Milk	45 ml	3 tbsp	3 tbsp
Stewed fruit such as prunes, figs or apples, mixed if liked	225 g	8 oz	8 oz

1 Sift the dry ingredients together into a bowl, then rub in the butter or margarine until the mixture resembles breadcrumbs.

2 Make a well in the centre and drop in the eggs (you do not need to beat them first). Mix to a thick batter with the milk.

3 Put the stewed fruit into a greased pie dish, then spoon over the batter. Bake in a preheated oven at 180°C/350°F/gas mark 4 for 30 minutes until firm and golden.

⏲ **Preparation and cooking time:** 40 minutes

Dundee Cake

SERVES 4

	METRIC	IMPERIAL	AMERICAN
Sultanas (golden raisins)	225 g	8 oz	1⅓ cups
Currants	225 g	8 oz	1⅓ cups
Chopped mixed (candied) peel	75 g	3 oz	½ cup
Brandy	15 ml	1 tbsp	1 tbsp
Caster (superfine) sugar	175 g	6 oz	¾ cup
Butter or margarine, softened	175 g	6 oz	¾ cup
Eggs	3	3	3
Plain (all-purpose) flour	225 g	8 oz	2 cups
Ground almonds	15 ml	1 tbsp	1 tbsp
Glacé (candied) cherries, halved	75 g	3 oz	⅓ cup
Rind and juice of ½ lemon			
A pinch of salt			
Baking powder	5 ml	1 tsp	1 tsp
Blanched almonds, halved	25 g	1 oz	2 tbsp
Milk	30 ml	2 tbsp	2 tbsp

1 Soak the dried fruit and mixed peel in the brandy while preparing the cake mixture.

2 Reserve 15 ml/1 tbsp of the sugar, then cream the remainder with the butter or margarine. Add the eggs one at a time, alternating with a good sprinkling of the flour and beating continuously.

3 Fold in the ground almonds, then add the soaked fruits and peel, the cherries and lemon rind and juice together with a pinch of salt. Sift the remaining flour with the baking powder over the surface and fold into the mixture.

4 Turn into a greased and lined 20 cm/8 in cake tin (pan). Cover loosely with foil and bake in a preheated oven at 150°C/300°F/gas mark 2 for 1¼ hours.

5 Remove the foil and arrange the almonds halves over, then return to the oven for a further 1¼ hours until a skewer inserted in the centre comes out clean. Cover with greaseproof paper if it is browning too quickly.

6 Bring the milk to the boil with the reserved sugar, then brush the mixture over the top and return to the oven for a further 5 minutes to glaze.

7 Leave to cool in the tin.

⊙ **Preparation and cooking time:** 2¾ hours

Forfar Shortbread

Do not be tempted to use margarine instead of butter when making shortbread – the flavour is never as good.

MAKES ABOUT 16 ROUNDS

	METRIC	IMPERIAL	AMERICAN
Butter	*350 g*	*12 oz*	*1½ cups*
Plain (all-purpose) flour	*450 g*	*1 lb*	*4 cups*
Rice flour	*50 g*	*2 oz*	*½ cup*
Caster (superfine) sugar	*75 g*	*3 oz*	*⅓ cup*

1 Rub the butter into the flours, then stir in the sugar.

2 Knead the mixture on a lightly floured surface until smooth. Shape into small rounds and place on greased baking (cookie) sheets.

3 Bake in a preheated oven at 180°C/350°F/gas mark 4 for about 20 minutes until golden brown. Transfer to a wire rack to cool, then store in an airtight container.

⊙ **Preparation and cooking time:** 35 minutes

Pitcaithly Bannock

SERVES 4

	METRIC	IMPERIAL	AMERICAN
Butter or margarine, softened	100 g	4 oz	½ cup
Caster (superfine) sugar, plus extra for sprinkling	50 g	2 oz	¼ cup
Plain (all-purpose) flour	225 g	8 oz	2 cups
Blanched almonds, finely chopped	25 g	1 oz	¼ cup
Finely grated orange or lemon rind	30 ml	2 tbsp	2 tbsp

1 Knead the butter or margarine and sugar together by hand on a board, then gradually work in the flour, almonds and citrus peel. Continue to knead until smooth.

2 Press into a round about 1 cm/½ in thick and place on a sheet of non-stick baking parchment or greased greaseproof (waxed) paper on a greased baking (cookie) sheet. Prick all over with a fork and bake in the centre of a preheated oven at 160°C/325°F/gas mark 3 for 45–50 minutes until light golden.

3 Sprinkle with caster sugar and leave to cool slightly before marking into wedges and placing on a wire rack to cool.

⏲ **Preparation and cooking time:** 1 hour

Petticoat Tails

SERVES 4

	METRIC	IMPERIAL	AMERICAN
Plain (all-purpose) flour	175 g	6 oz	1½ cups
Caraway seeds	15 g	½ oz	2 tbsp
Butter, softened	100 g	4 oz	½ cup
Caster (superfine) sugar	50 g	2 oz	¼ cup
Icing (confectioners') sugar, for dusting			

1 Mix the flour with the caraway seeds, make a well in the centre and gradually knead in the softened butter or margarine with the caster sugar to bind together. Do not allow the mixture to become soft and oily.

2 Roll out thinly on a lightly floured surface, then invert a dinner plate on to the paste as a guide and run a pastry wheel around it to cut out a round. Mark another, smaller circle inside it, using a saucer or tumbler as a guide. Do not remove the inner circle, but mark the outer ring into eight 'petticoat tails'.

3 Place on a greased and lined baking (cookie) sheet and bake in a preheated oven at 150°C/300°F/gas mark 2 for 20–30 minutes until pale golden brown and crisp.

4 Leave to cool, then dust with icing sugar and serve.

🕒 **Preparation and cooking time:** 45 minutes

Hamilton Gingerbread

MAKES ONE 23 CM/9 IN CAKE

	METRIC	IMPERIAL	AMERICAN
Self-raising (self-rising) flour	450 g	1 lb	4 cups
Ground ginger	10 ml	2 tsp	2 tsp
Butter or margarine	175 g	6 oz	¾ cup
Light brown sugar	175 g	6 oz	¾ cup
Black treacle (molasses)	175 g	6 oz	½ cup
Bicarbonate of soda (baking soda)	5 ml	1 tsp	1 tsp
Milk	45 ml	3 tbsp	3 tbsp

1 Mix together the flour and ginger.

2 Cream together the butter or margarine, sugar and treacle, then work into the flour mixture.

3 Mix the bicarbonate of soda with a little water, then stir it into the mixture with enough of the milk to give a soft, dropping consistency.

4 Spoon into a greased and lined 23 cm/9 in cake tin (pan) and bake in a preheated oven at 180°C/350°F/gas mark 4 for 1½ hours until springy to the touch.

5 Leave to cool, then cut into squares.

⏲ **Preparation and cooking time:** 1¾ hours

Tantallon Cakes

Serves 4

	METRIC	IMPERIAL	AMERICAN
Plain (all-purpose) flour	*450 g*	*1 lb*	*4 cups*
Rice flour	*15 ml*	*1 tbsp*	*1 tbsp*
Butter or margarine	*225 g*	*8 oz*	*1 cup*
Caster (superfine) sugar,			
* plus extra for sprinkling*	*50 g*	*2 oz*	*¼ cup*

1 Sift the flours into a bowl, then rub in the butter or margarine until the mixture resembles fine breadcrumbs. Stir in the sugar and work together with your hands until it forms a soft ball.

2 Place on a lightly floured board and use your hands to press it out to 1 cm/½ in thick. Cut into small circles with a biscuit (cookie) cutter and place on a greased baking (cookie) sheet.

3 Bake in a preheated oven at 180°C/350°F/gas mark 4 for about 30 minutes until golden brown.

4 Leave to cool, then serve sprinkled with a little caster sugar.

⊙ **Preparation and cooking time:** 45 minutes

Queen Mary Tartlets

For extra flavour, add 5 ml/1 tsp finely grated lemon rind.

MAKES 12

	METRIC	IMPERIAL	AMERICAN
Plain (all-purpose) flour	100 g	4 oz	1 cup
A pinch of salt			
Butter or margarine	75 g	3 oz	⅓ cup
Caster (superfine) sugar	5 ml	1 tsp	1 tsp
Egg yolk	1	1	1
For the filling:			
Caster (superfine) sugar	50 g	2 oz	¼ cup
Butter or margarine	50 g	2 oz	¼ cup
Egg	1	1	1
Chopped mixed (candied) peel	25 g	1 oz	3 tbsp
Sultanas (golden raisins)	100 g	4 oz	⅔ cup

1 Sift the flour and salt into a bowl and rub in the butter or margarine until the mixture resembles fine breadcrumbs. Stir in the sugar.

2 Mix the egg yolk with 30 ml/2 tbsp of cold water and add to the mixture, then knead to a dough. Roll out thinly on a lightly floured board, cut into rounds with a biscuit (cookie) cutter and use to line 12 tartlet tins (patty pans).

3 To make the filling, cream together the sugar and butter or margarine, then beat in the egg. Add the mixed peel and sultanas, then divide the mixture between the tart cases (pie shells).

4 Bake in a preheated oven at 190°C/375°F/gas mark 5 for 30–35 minutes until golden and set.

5 Leave to cool before serving.

🕐 **Preparation and cooking time:** 45 minutes

Edinburgh Scones

Makes 8–10

	METRIC	IMPERIAL	AMERICAN
Self-raising (self-rising) flour	275 g	10 oz	2½ cups
A pinch of salt			
Baking powder	10 ml	2 tsp	2 tsp
Caster (superfine) sugar	10 ml	2 tsp	2 tsp
Butter or margarine	50 g	2 oz	¼ cup
Currants	75 g	3 oz	½ cup
Egg, beaten	1	1	1
Milk	150 ml	¼ pt	⅔ cup
Butter, to serve			

1 Mix together the flour, salt, baking powder and sugar. Rub in the butter or margarine until the mixture resembles breadcrumbs, then add the currants.

2 Blend in the egg and enough of the milk to make a soft but not sticky dough; you may not need to use all the milk. Knead on a lightly floured board until smooth.

3 Roll out to about 1 cm/½ in thick and cut into rounds with a pastry (cookie) cutter. Place on a greased baking (cookie) sheet and bake in a preheated oven at 220°C/425°F/gas mark 7 for about 10 minutes until light golden brown and the bases sound hollow when tapped.

4 Leave to cool on a wire rack, then serve split and buttered.

⏲ **Preparation and cooking time:** 20 minutes

Edinburgh Rock

This recipe makes green mint and yellow lemon rock, but you can experiment with many different colours and flavours.

MAKES ABOUT 450 G/1 LB

	METRIC	IMPERIAL	AMERICAN
Loaf sugar	450 g	1 lb	2 cups
Water	150 ml	¼ pt	⅔ cup
Cream of tartar	1.5 ml	¼ tsp	¼ tsp
Green and yellow food colouring			
Peppermint and lemon flavouring			
Oil, for greasing			

1 Put the sugar and water in a heavy-based saucepan. Heat gently, stirring occasionally, until the sugar has completely dissolved.

2 Bring almost to the boil, then stir in the cream of tartar. Boil until the mixture reaches 122°C/252°F on a sugar thermometer, or until a teaspoon of the mixture forms a hard ball when dropped into a cup of cold water.

3 Pour half the mixture into a separate heatproof bowl. Stir enough green food colouring into one and yellow food colouring into the other to give a delicate shade. Add a few drops of peppermint flavouring to the green, and lemon flavouring to the yellow, and mix each one well.

4 Pour the peppermint mixture into one oiled, shallow baking tin (pan) and the lemon mixture into another. As the edges cool, turn them towards the centre, using an oiled knife.

5 When the mixture is cool enough to handle, start to pull and fold the mixture, then pull into a long sausage shape, about 1 cm/½ in thick.

6 Cut into short sticks with scissors. Arrange on a sheet of non-stick baking parchment and leave to stand for about 24 hours until crumbly. Store in an airtight container.

⏲ **Preparation and cooling time:** 35 minutes

Butterscotch

MAKES ABOUT 450 G/1 LB

	METRIC	IMPERIAL	AMERICAN
Water	150 ml	¼ pt	⅔ cup
Lemon juice	5 ml	1 tsp	1 tsp
Granulated sugar	450 g	1 lb	2 cups
Cream of tartar	1.5 ml	¼ tsp	¼ tsp
Unsalted (sweet) butter, cut			
into small pieces	75 g	3 oz	⅓ cup
Vanilla essence (extract)	1.5 ml	¼ tsp	¼ tsp
Oil, for greasing			

1 Thoroughly oil a 28 × 18 cm/11 × 7 in shallow baking tin (pan).

2 Put the water and lemon juice in a heavy-based saucepan and heat until slightly warm. Stir in the sugar and continue to heat gently, stirring with a wooden spoon, until all the sugar has completely dissolved. There should not be even the slightest feeling of grittiness when you stir. Do not allow to boil.

3 Stir in the cream of tartar, then bring to the boil and boil to 115°C/242°F on a sugar thermometer or until a teaspoonful of the mixture forms a soft ball when dropped into a cup of cold water.

4 Remove from the heat and beat in the butter. Return to the heat and boil to 138°C/280°F, when a teaspoonful of the mixture forms a thin thread when dropped into a cup of cold water. The thread will bend and break when pressed between your fingers.

5 Remove from the heat and beat in the vanilla essence, then pour into the oiled tin and leave until almost set. Mark into small oblongs with a knife.

6 When completely set, break into pieces and store in an airtight container.

⏱ **Preparation and cooking time:** 30 minutes plus setting

Dundee Marmalade

MAKES ABOUT 3.5 KG/8 LB

	METRIC	IMPERIAL	AMERICAN
Seville oranges	1 kg	2¼ lb	2¼ lb
Lemons	2	2	2
Water	4.75 litres	8 pts	20 cups
Preserving sugar	2 kg	4 lb	8 cups

1 Wash the fruit thoroughly, place in a large saucepan with the water and cover. Simmer for about 1 hour until the skins are soft enough to be easily pierced.

2 Cut the fruit into small pieces in a bowl, and pour off into a pan the juice. Separate the pips and tie loosely in muslin (cheesecloth) or a new disposable kitchen cloth. Place in a pan with the juice and boil together for 15 minutes, then strain the juice into a large preserving pan.

3 Add the sugar and fruit, stir until the sugar is completely dissolved, then bring to the boil and boil rapidly, without stirring, to setting point (110°C /220°F). To test if setting point is reached, place a small spoonful on a cold saucer: it should wrinkle when pushed with your finger.

4 Remove any scum, leave to cool slightly, then spoon into clean, warmed jars. Leave to cool completely, then cover and store in a cool, dark place.

🕐 **Preparation and cooking time:** 2 hours

The Borders

The sedate Border country is the land of romance and poets where a tasteful, leisurely lifestyle with simple but elegant dishes has evolved from the richness of the soil and the beauty of the rivers.

The Tweed is justifiably famous for its delicious salmon. Like grouse, salmon can be served with sauces and other garnishes, but the locals prefer it as plain as possible with little to distract from its natural taste.

Here the emphasis on farming has always been very great. The landowners were traditionally renowned for taking care of their workers, making sure that they were well housed, and well fed on nutritious dishes such as Galloway Hot-pot (see page 111) and Sassermaet (see page 113).

Salmon Trimmings Soup

The Scots are renowned for their thriftiness and this dish is one of the most brilliant ways of using the bits of fish many people would throw away. It's worth asking your fishmonger for the 'bits' if you aren't buying whole fish.

SERVES 6

	METRIC	IMPERIAL	AMERICAN
Head and end of tailpiece of 1 salmon			
Head and bones of 1 plaice or sole			
Water	1.5 litres	2½ pts	6 cups
Bouquet garni sachet	1	1	1
Salt and freshly ground black pepper			
Large carrot, finely diced	1	1	1
Bunch of spring onions (scallions), chopped	1	1	1
Celery stick, chopped	1	1	1
Potato, chopped	1	1	1
Large ripe tomatoes, skinned, seeded and chopped	2	2	2
Milk	300 ml	½ pt	1¼ cups
Cornflour (cornstarch)	15 ml	1 tbsp	1 tbsp
Double (heavy) cream	75 ml	5 tbsp	5 tbsp
Scotch whisky	30 ml	2 tbsp	2 tbsp

1 Put the fish heads, tails and bones, the water, bouquet garni and some salt and pepper in a large saucepan. Bring to the boil, skim the surface, reduce the heat, cover and simmer gently for 1 hour.

2 Strain and return the stock to the rinsed-out saucepan.

3 Pick all the meat out of the heads and tails and return to the pan. Add all the prepared vegetables, bring to the boil, reduce the heat and simmer for 30 minutes until really tender.

4 Purée in a blender or food processor and return to the pan.

5 Blend the milk with the cornflour and stir in. Bring to the boil, then reduce the heat and simmer for 1 minute, stirring. Stir in the cream and whisky, taste and adjust the seasoning if necessary. No garnish is needed.

🕐 **Preparation and cooking time:** 1¾ hours

Spiced Salmon

SERVES 4

	METRIC	IMPERIAL	AMERICAN
Piece of salmon	*900 g*	*2 lb*	*2 lb*
Cayenne	*1.5 ml*	*¼ tsp*	*¼ tsp*
Whole allspice	*10 ml*	*2 tsp*	*2 tsp*
Whole cloves	*8*	*8*	*8*
Ground mace	*5 ml*	*1 tsp*	*1 tsp*
Salt	*20 ml*	*4 tsp*	*4 tsp*
Wine vinegar	*1.2 litres*	*2 pts*	*5 cups*
Mixed leaf salad, to serve			

1 Lay the salmon on a rack in a fish kettle or on a piece of foil, leaving a large enough flap at each side to lift it out. Poach in simmering water for about 15 minutes until just tender. Remove from the pan.

2 Cut the fish into slices and arrange in an earthenware casserole dish (Dutch oven). Sprinkle the slices with the spices and a little salt. Pour over the vinegar, making sure that the fish is completely covered, and leave to stand for at least 24 hours.

3 Pour off any excess liquor into a sauce boat. Serve the salmon and spicy sauce with a mixed leaf salad.

🕐 **Preparation and cooking time:** 20 minutes plus standing

Baked Salmon Steaks

SERVES 4

	METRIC	IMPERIAL	AMERICAN
Salmon steaks	4	4	4
Unsalted (sweet) butter	50 g	2 oz	¼ cup
Salt and freshly ground black pepper			

1 Cut four large squares of foil and place a steak in the centre of each one. Dot generously with butter and season with salt and pepper to taste. Seal the tops.

2 Bake in a preheated oven 160°C/325°F/gas mark 3 for 20 minutes until perfectly tender.

3 Serve in their own juices, either hot or cold.

🕐 **Preparation and cooking time:** 30 minutes

Grilled Salmon Steaks

SERVES 4

	METRIC	IMPERIAL	AMERICAN
Salmon steaks	4	4	4
Olive oil	30 ml	2 tbsp	2 tbsp
Lemon juice	20 ml	4 tsp	4 tsp
Salt and freshly ground black pepper			
Unsalted (sweet) butter, to serve			

1 Place the steaks on the grill (broiler) rack, brush with olive oil and lemon juice on both sides, and season with salt and pepper. Leave to stand for 20 minutes.

2 Grill (broil), turning once, under a moderate heat for 5–10 minutes, depending on thickness, until tender and just cooked. Dot with butter, then serve.

🕐 **Preparation and cooking time:** 25–30 minutes

Kale Brose

*This dish was once one of the staple foods of Scotland. It was
generally made with water for breakfast and with stock for the
evening meal. There are many variations but this is one of
the most popular.*

SERVES 4

	METRIC	IMPERIAL	AMERICAN
Oatmeal	50 g	2 oz	¼ cup
Stock	1.75 litres	3 pts	7½ cups
Large onion, chopped	1	1	1
Dripping or lard (shortening)	15 g	½ oz	1 tbsp
Green kale, shredded	450 g	1 lb	1 lb
Salt and freshly ground black pepper			
Scottish Oatcakes (see page 124), to serve			

1 Place the oatmeal and half the stock in a saucepan,
bring to the boil, then reduce the heat and simmer for
30 minutes. Gradually add the remaining stock, stirring
rapidly as you pour until thinned to taste.

2 Fry (sauté) the onion in the dripping or lard for
3 minutes. Stir into the oatmeal broth.

3 Add the kale and simmer for a further 30 minutes.
Season to taste with salt and pepper and serve with Scottish
Oatcakes.

⏱ **Preparation and cooking time:** 40 minutes

Scotch Woodcock

There are several variations of this dish. This one is particularly rich and creamy.

SERVES 4

	METRIC	IMPERIAL	AMERICAN
Butter or margarine	150 g	5 oz	⅔ cup
Anchovy fillets, rinsed	8	8	8
Egg yolks	4	4	4
Double (heavy) cream	75 ml	5 tbsp	5 tbsp
Chopped fresh parsley	15 ml	1 tbsp	1 tbsp
Salt and freshly ground black pepper			
Slices of hot toast	4	4	4

1 Thoroughly mash 75 g/3 oz/⅓ cup of the butter or margarine with the anchovies until blended, then chill until required.

2 Melt the remaining butter or margarine in the top of a double boiler, or in a bowl over a pan of simmering water, and add the egg yolks, cream and parsley. Stir with a wooden spoon for a few minutes until it thickens, then season to taste with salt and pepper.

3 Spread the slices of toast with the anchovy butter and pour over the hot sauce.

🕐 **Preparation and cooking time:** 20 minutes

Galloway Hot-pot

You may like to make any remaining stock into gravy to accompany the hot-pot.

SERVES 4

	METRIC	IMPERIAL	AMERICAN
Neck of mutton or lamb	900 g	2 lb	2 lb
Onion, halved	1	1	1
Potatoes, sliced	900 g	2 lb	2 lb
Sheep's kidneys, skinned, cored and sliced	3	3	3
Salt and freshly ground black pepper			
Butter or margarine	25 g	1 oz	2 tbsp

1 Trim the fat and bones off the meat and divide into cutlets. Put the fat trimmings, short rib bones and onion into a large saucepan and cover with water. Bring to the boil, then simmer for 1 hour to make a stock. Drain, reserving the liquid.

2 Put a layer of sliced potatoes in the bottom of a casserole dish (Dutch oven). Arrange the cutlets slightly overlapping on top. Cover with the sliced kidneys. Season well with salt and pepper and repeat the layers, ending with a layer of potatoes.

3 Pour 300 ml/½ pt/1¼ cups of the reserved stock carefully down the side, so as not to soak the potatoes. Dot with butter or margarine, then cover and bake in a preheated oven at 180°C/350°F/gas mark 4 for 2 hours. Remove the cover, then return to the oven for 30 minutes until cooked through and golden.

⏲ **Preparation and cooking time:** 3 hours

Royal Game Pie

SERVES 4

	METRIC	IMPERIAL	AMERICAN
Large cock pheasant	1	1	1
OR Pigeons	3	3	3
Plain (all-purpose) flour	25 g	1 oz	¼ cup
Salt and freshly ground black pepper			
Mushrooms, sliced	175 g	6 oz	6 oz
Large onion, sliced	1	1	1
Streaky bacon rashers (slices), rinded and chopped	5	5	5
Chopped fresh parsley	15 ml	1 tbsp	1 tbsp
A pinch of dried mixed herbs			
Stock	120 ml	¼ pt	⅔ cup
Red wine or port	120 ml	¼ pt	⅔ cup
Puff pastry (paste), thawed if frozen	225 g	8 oz	8 oz
A little beaten egg, to glaze			

1 Cut the game into joints. Season the flour with salt and freshly ground black pepper and toss the meat in the flour, then arrange in a large pie dish. Add the mushrooms, onion, bacon, parsley and herbs. Pour the stock and wine or port over, then season with salt and pepper.

2 Roll out the pastry on a lightly floured surface and make a 'lid' slightly larger than the pie. Cut off a strip all round. Brush the rim of the dish with water and put the strip on the rim. Dampen again and lay the pastry lid on top. Knock up and flute with the back of a knife.

3 Make a hole in the centre to allow the steam to escape. Decorate with leaves made out of the pastry trimmings and brush with the beaten egg.

4 Bake in a preheated oven at 220°C/425°F/gas mark 7 for 20 minutes, then reduce the oven temperature to 160°C/325°F/gas mark 3 for a further 2 hours. Cover loosely with greaseproof (waxed) paper or foil for the last 30 minutes to prevent it from over-browning.

⏲ **Preparation and cooking time:** 3 hours

Sassermaet

Although it is totally unauthentic, these patties are delicious served with slices of fried (sautéed) aubergine (eggplant) and a fresh tomato and Feta cheese salad.

SERVES 4

	METRIC	IMPERIAL	AMERICAN
Lean minced (ground) beef	450 g	1 lb	1 lb
Shredded (chopped) beef suet	225 g	8 oz	2 cups
Ground cinnamon	5 ml	1 tsp	1 tsp
Ground cloves	5 ml	1 tsp	1 tsp
Mixed (apple-pie) spice	5 ml	1 tsp	1 tsp
Ground ginger	5 ml	1 tsp	1 tsp
Ground mace	2.5 ml	½ tsp	½ tsp
Light brown sugar	5 ml	1 tsp	1 tsp
Salt and freshly ground black pepper			

1 Mix the beef and suet together in a bowl.

2 Add the remaining ingredients, seasoning well with salt and pepper. Work together with your hands until thoroughly blended.

3 Shape the mixture into eight brunies (small round cakes) and dry-fry very gently for about 20 minutes, turning occasionally until golden brown and cooked through.

⏲ **Preparation and cooking time:** 25 minutes

Nettle Haggis

Use enough nettles to fill a medium-sized saucepan.

SERVES 4

	METRIC	IMPERIAL	AMERICAN
Young nettle tops (see above)			
Boiling water	600 ml	1 pt	2½ cups
Bacon rashers (slices), rinded	3	3	3
Medium oatmeal	45 ml	3 tbsp	3 tbsp
Salt and freshly ground black pepper			

1 Wash the nettles well, place in a saucepan and pour on the boiling water. Return to the boil and boil quickly, uncovered, for about 10 minutes until very tender. Strain, reserving 300 ml/½ pt/1¼ cups of the water. Chop the nettles as you would spinach and return to the pan.

2 Fry (sauté) the bacon until crisp. Pour the bacon fat over the nettles in the saucepan.

3 Pour the reserved nettle water into a second saucepan. Bring to the boil and gradually add the oatmeal, stirring constantly. Season well with salt and pepper. Lower the heat and keep stirring with a wooden spoon until quite thick, then turn into a double boiler or a bowl placed over a pan of simmering water. Cover and cook for 30 minutes, stirring occasionally.

4 Stir in the nettles, season to taste with salt and pepper and crumble the bacon over the top. Serve at once.

⏱ **Preparation and cooking time:** 1 hour

Melrose Pudding

SERVES 4–6

	METRIC	IMPERIAL	AMERICAN
Butter or margarine, plus extra for greasing	100 g	4 oz	½ cup
Caster (superfine) sugar	100 g	4 oz	½ cup
Plain (all-purpose) flour	225 g	8 oz	2 cups
Eggs, beaten	2	2	2
Baking powder	5 ml	1 tsp	1 tsp
Ground almonds	50 g	2 oz	½ cup
Milk	150 ml	¼ pt	⅔ cup
Glacé (candied) cherries, halved	50 g	2 oz	¼ cup
Raisins	75 g	3 oz	½ cup
Creamy custard or chocolate sauce, to serve			

1 Cream the butter or margarine and the sugar in a large bowl, then gradually add the flour, a spoonful at a time, alternating with spoonfuls of beaten egg. Add the baking powder with the last spoonful of flour and beat well. Stir in the almonds and enough of the milk to make a soft batter.

2 Arrange the cherries and raisins decoratively around the base of a greased 1.2 litre/2 pt/5 cup pudding basin, then spoon in the batter.

3 Cover with a double thickness of greased and pleated greaseproof (waxed) paper, twisting and folding to secure, and place the basin on an old saucer or trivet in a saucepan. Pour in enough boiling water to come halfway up the sides of the basin, then cover and simmer for 1½ hours, topping up with boiling water as necessary.

4 Leave to cool for a couple of minutes before carefully turning out. Serve hot with creamy custard or chocolate sauce.

🕑 **Preparation and cooking time:** 2 hours

Melrose Creams

SERVES 4

	METRIC	IMPERIAL	AMERICAN
Can of pineapple rings, drained	225 g	8 oz	1 medium
Can of apricots	400 g	14 oz	1 large
Double (heavy) cream	300 ml	½ pt	1¼ cups
Glacé (candied) cherries, quartered	12	12	12
Single (light) cream	300 ml	½ pt	1¼ cups
Plain (semi-sweet) chocolate, grated	50 g	2 oz	½ cup

1 Cut each pineapple ring into six equal pieces. Rub the apricots through a sieve (strainer) into a bowl or purée in a blender or food processor.

2 Whisk the double cream until softly peaking, then stir in the cherries. Gradually whisk in the apricot purée until it is all blended in with the cream.

3 Divide the pineapple equally between six small glass dishes. Spoon the apricot fool over and chill.

4 Top with a thin layer of single cream and sprinkle generously with grated chocolate.

🕐 **Preparation time:** 20 minutes plus chilling

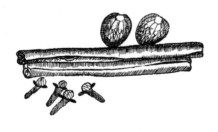

Flummery

Start this dessert three days before you need it. You can try using lemons instead of oranges for a really tangy alternative.

SERVES 6

	METRIC	IMPERIAL	AMERICAN
Fine oatmeal	75 g	3 oz	¾ cup
Coarsely grated rind and juice of 2 oranges			
Caster (superfine) sugar	25 g	1 oz	2 tbsp
Double (heavy) cream	300 ml	½ pt	1¼ cups
Clear Scottish heather honey	30 ml	2 tbsp	2 tbsp

1 Put the oatmeal in a bowl and just cover with cold water. Cover and leave to stand for 24 hours, adding a little more water as necessary to keep the oatmeal covered.

2 Strain off the liquid and tip the oatmeal back into the bowl. Pour over 1.2 litres/2 pts/5 cups fresh water and leave to stand for a further 24 hours.

3 Strain through a sieve (strainer) into a saucepan, pressing the oatmeal with a wooden spoon to extract as much liquid as possible. Discard the oatmeal.

4 Strain the orange juice and put in the saucepan with the sugar, stirring to dissolve the sugar. Bring to the boil, reduce the heat and simmer for 10 minutes until thick, stirring all the time.

5 Remove from the heat and leave until fairly cool, then stir in half the cream. Pour into six individual serving dishes and leave to set.

6 Whip the remaining cream until peaking. Top each flummery with a spoonful of the whipped cream, trickle the honey over and sprinkle with the orange rind.

⏱ **Preparation and cooking time:** 20 minutes plus standing and setting

Whim-wham

SERVES 4

	METRIC	IMPERIAL	AMERICAN
Puff pastry (paste), thawed if frozen	225 g	8 oz	8 oz
Redcurrant jelly (clear conserve)	100 g	4 oz	½ cup
Double (heavy) cream	750 ml	1½ pts	3¾ cups
Caster (superfine) sugar	10 ml	2 tsp	2 tsp
White wine	120 ml	4 fl oz	½ cup
Grated rind of 1 lemon			
Crystallised (candied) orange and lemon slices, to decorate			

1 Divide the pastry in half, roll out and cut into two rounds slightly smaller than the diameter of a deep glass dessert dish. Place on a dampened baking (cookie) sheet and bake in a preheated oven at 230°C/450°F/gas mark 8 for about 10 minutes until risen, crisp and golden. Leave to cool.

2 Spread the cold pastry with redcurrant jelly.

3 Whip the cream with the sugar, wine and lemon rind until thick, then spoon one-third into the dessert dish. Cover with a round of pastry. Repeat the layers, finishing with the cream. Decorate with crystallised fruit slices.

🕐 **Preparation time:** 30 minutes

Apple Fruit Cake

SERVES 4

	METRIC	IMPERIAL	AMERICAN
Caster (superfine) sugar	100 g	4 oz	½ cup
Butter or margarine	100 g	4 oz	½ cup
Self-raising (self-rising) flour	225 g	8 oz	2 cups
Ground cinnamon	5 ml	1 tsp	1 tsp
Ground ginger	2.5 ml	½ tsp	½ tsp
Mixed (apple-pie) spice	2.5 ml	½ tsp	½ tsp
Sultanas (golden raisins)	100 g	4 oz	⅔ cup
Malt vinegar	15 ml	1 tbsp	1 tbsp
Apple purée (apple sauce)	300 ml	½ pt	1¼ cups

1 Cream the sugar with the butter or margarine, then gradually add all the dry ingredients. Finally add the vinegar and apple purée.

2 Pour the mixture into a greased and lined 20 cm/8 in cake tin (pan) and bake in a preheated oven at 180°C/350°F/gas mark 4 for about 1½ hours until a skewer inserted in the centre comes out clean.

3 Leave to cool before serving.

🕐 **Preparation and cooking time:** 2 hours

Black Bun

Black Bun is traditionally served at New Year and is best made a few months beforehand to allow the cake to mature. Store in an airtight container.

SERVES 4

	METRIC	IMPERIAL	AMERICAN
Shortcrust pastry (basic pie crust)	400 g	14 oz	14 oz
Large raisins, stoned	450 g	1 lb	2⅔ cups
Sultanas (golden raisins)	225 g	8 oz	1⅓ cups
Currants	225 g	8 oz	1⅓ cups
Chopped mixed (candied) peel	50 g	2 oz	⅓ cup
Blanched almonds	100 g	4 oz	1 cup
Plain (all-purpose) flour	225 g	8 oz	2 cups
Ground cinnamon	5 ml	1 tsp	1 tsp
Ground ginger	2.5 ml	½ tsp	½ tsp
Grated nutmeg	2.5 ml	½ tsp	½ tsp
Mixed (apple-pie) spice	2.5 ml	½ tsp	½ tsp
Cream of tartar	5 ml	1 tsp	1 tsp
Bicarbonate of soda (baking soda)	5 ml	1 tsp	1 tsp
Light brown sugar	100 g	4 oz	½ cup
Egg, beaten	1	1	1
Scotch whisky	120 ml	4 fl oz	½ cup
Milk	60 ml	4 tbsp	4 tbsp
Beaten egg, to glaze			

1 Roll out three-quarters of the pastry (paste) on a lightly floured surface and use to line a 20 cm/8 in round cake tin (pan), making sure that the pastry comes at least 2.5 cm/1 in above the top of the sides of the tin.

2 Mix together all the remaining ingredients, beating until smooth, then pack into the pastry case (pie shell). Fold the pastry over the top of the filling but do not push down or try to enclose completely.

3 Roll out the remaining pastry to a 20 cm/8 in round,

moisten the edges and seal over the pastry case to make a lid. Make several holes with a fine skewer through to the base of the cake, then prick the lid all over with a fork. Brush with the beaten egg.

4 Bake in the centre of a preheated oven at 180°C/ 350°F/gas mark 4 for 2½–3 hours until a skewer inserted in the centre comes out clean. Cover loosely with foil after 45 minutes to prevent over-browning.

🕐 **Preparation and cooking time:** 3½ hours

Oatmeal Bannocks

MAKES 6

	METRIC	IMPERIAL	AMERICAN
Wholemeal flour	175 g	6 oz	1½ cups
Baking powder	15 ml	1 tbsp	1 tbsp
Salt	2.5 ml	½ tsp	½ tsp
Butter or margarine, plus			
extra for spreading	25 g	1 oz	2 tbsp
Fine oatmeal	50 g	2 oz	½ cup
Caster (superfine) sugar	15 g	½ oz	1 tbsp
Water	150 ml	¼ pt	⅔ cup

1 Mix together the flour, baking powder and salt.

2 Rub in the butter or margarine and stir in the oatmeal and sugar. Mix with enough of the water to form a soft but not sticky dough.

3 Knead gently on a lightly floured surface. Divide the mixture into six equal pieces and shape each into a small, flat cake, about 1 cm/½ in thick.

4 Heat a griddle or non-stick, heavy-based frying pan (skillet) and cook the bannocks for about 5 minutes on each side until risen and golden. Serve warm, split and spread with butter or margarine.

🕐 **Preparation and cooking time:** 20 minutes

Barley Bannocks

SERVES 4

	METRIC	IMPERIAL	AMERICAN
Barley meal	225 g	8 oz	2 cups
Plain (all-purpose) flour	50 g	2 oz	½ cup
A large pinch of salt			
Bicarbonate of soda (baking soda)	5 ml	1 tsp	1 tsp
Buttermilk	450 ml	¾ pt	2 cups

1 Mix the barley meal, flour and salt in a bowl.

2 Whisk the bicarbonate of soda into the buttermilk. When it begins to froth, pour into the dry ingredients and mix to a soft dough, handling it as little as possible.

3 Roll out gently on a lightly floured surface into a circle 1 cm/½ in thick and cut into rounds with a 7.5 cm/3 in biscuit (cookie) cutter.

4 Place on a hot griddle or in a heavy-based frying pan (skillet) and cook for about 5 minutes until well risen and brown underneath, then turn and brown other side. When the edges are dry, they are ready.

5 Alternatively, place on a greased baking (cookie) sheet and brush with milk. Bake in a preheated oven at 220°C/425°F/gas mark 7 for 10–12 minutes.

6 Leave to cool on a wire rack.

🕐 **Preparation and cooking time:** 25 minutes

Selkirk Bannock

SERVES 4

	METRIC	IMPERIAL	AMERICAN
Strong white plain (bread) flour	275 g	10 oz	2½ cups
Caster (superfine) sugar	12.5 ml	2½ tsp	2½ tsp
A pinch of salt			
Butter or margarine	25 g	1 oz	2 tbsp
Easy-blend dried yeast	10 ml	2 tsp	2 tsp
Egg, beaten	1	1	1
Warm milk	150 ml	¼ pt	⅔ cup
Sultanas (golden raisins)	50 g	2 oz	⅓ cup
Currants	50 g	2 oz	⅓ cup
Chopped mixed (candied) peel	25 g	1 oz	3 tbsp
Beaten egg, to glaze			

1 Sift the flour, 2.5 ml/½ tsp of sugar and the salt into a warmed bowl, then rub in the butter or margarine. Stir in the yeast.

2 Using a wooden spoon, beat the egg and milk into the mixture to form a dough.

3 Add the fruit and peel, knead well and place in an oiled polythene bag. Tie loosely and leave to rise in a warm place for about 1 hour until doubled in size and springy to the touch. Knead again.

4 Shape to fit a greased 20 cm/8 in round, shallow cake tin (pan). Using a sharp knife, score the top into eight sections and leave in a warm place to prove for about 1 hour until the dough is well risen again.

5 Brush with beaten egg, then bake in a preheated oven at 200°C/400°F/gas mark 6 for 35 minutes.

6 For a sticky coating, dissolve the remaining sugar in 15 ml/1 tbsp of water. Brush the bannock with this mixture as soon as it is removed from the oven.

⏲ **Preparation and cooking time:** 50 minutes plus rising

Scottish Oatcakes

MAKES 16

	METRIC	IMPERIAL	AMERICAN
Fine oatmeal	225 g	8 oz	2 cups
A pinch of salt			
A pinch of bicarbonate of soda (baking soda)			
Melted lard (shortening)	45 ml	3 tbsp	3 tbsp
Warm water	45 ml	3 tbsp	3 tbsp
Milk	45 ml	3 tbsp	3 tbsp
Butter or margarine and cheese, to serve			

1 Mix the dry ingredients together in a bowl. Add the melted lard or dripping, the water and enough milk to form a soft but not sticky dough.

2 Knead gently on a lightly floured surface. Cut in half. Roll out one half thinly and cut into a 20 cm/8 in round. Cut the round into eight wedges.

3 Repeat with the other piece of dough.

4 Place the oatcakes on a lightly greased baking (cookie) sheet and bake in a preheated oven at 180°/350°F/gas mark 4 for about 25–30 minutes until lightly golden and curling slightly at the edges. Cool on a wire rack. Store in an airtight container.

5 Serve split and buttered, with cheese.

☉ **Preparation and cooking time:** 45 minutes

Index